J. KRISHNAMURTI

Teacher, thinker, writer, and speaker, J. Krishnamurti (1895–1986) was an Indian educationist, spiritual leader, and key figure in world philosophy. He raised significant questions about the state of the world, about our tendency to remain passive, conditioned, and in a state of overwhelming confusion about how we relate to the world. Through talks and writings spread over many decades and geographical locations, he articulated an unconditioned, reflective approach which emphasised self-inquiry.

This volume provides an understanding of Krishnamurti's views on the human predicament in a disintegrating world, marked by conflict, divisions, wars, and climate change. It also examines his educational thought and its enormous potential for change. Krishnamurti argued that our minds are so conditioned that we are unable to look, listen, or learn without our prior knowledge that foregrounds the role of memory and time. He highlighted the need to work with young children, with a special focus on the school as the centrepiece of his perception for psychological development and educational excellence. It is within an educational setting that Krishnamurti hoped that the seeds for individual and social change will be catalysed.

An introspective look at the life and legacy of an eminent twentieth-century thinker, this volume will be of great interest to students and researchers of philosophy, education, religion and spirituality, South Asia studies, modern history, and the social sciences.

Meenakshi Thapan is a trustee of the Krishnamurti Foundation of India and currently the Director of the Rishi Valley Education Centre in rural Andhra Pradesh. She encountered Krishnamurti and his teachings very early in her life, and from then on, has had an ongoing engagement with his educational thought as well as institutions. She taught briefly at the Rishi Valley School and later conducted her doctoral field research within this school community, resulting in the publication of her first book, *Life at School: an ethnographic study* (1991, 2006, 2nd ed.). Subsequently, she has been a highly accomplished academician, based at the University of Delhi, and held the positions of Professor of Sociology and Director, Delhi School of Economics as well as Head of the D.S. Kothari Centre for Science, Ethics and Education, University of Delhi until her retirement in 2019.

Dr. Thapan has travelled widely, teaching, speaking, and contributing to university departments all over the world. She is the recipient of a number of prestigious awards, apart from being the author of numerous books, research papers, and articles in several prominent publications. The most recent are (ed.) *J. Krishnamurti and Educational Practice: Social and Moral Vision for Inclusive Education* (2018), *Education and Society: Themes, Perspectives, Practices* (ed.) (2015), *Ethnographies of Schooling in Contemporary India* (ed.) (2014), and *Contested Spaces: Citizenship and Belonging in Contemporary Times* (ed.) (2010).

PEACEMAKERS
Series Editor: Ramin Jahanbegloo,
Executive Director of the Mahatma Gandhi Centre for Nonviolence and Peace Studies and the Vice-Dean of the School of Law at Jindal Global University, India

Peace is one of the central concepts in the spiritual and political life of humanity. Peace does not imply the absence of war. It implies harmony, justice and empathy. Empathy is the key to education of peace in our world. In other words, despite the vast differences of values between cultures and traditions, it is still possible to grasp an understanding of one another, by 'empathy'. Throughout centuries, peacemakers have endorsed a 'shared human horizon' which according to them had the critical force of avoiding moral anarchy and relativism while acknowledging the plurality of modes of being human.

Today in a different manner and in a changed tone, but with the same moral courage and dissenting voice, this series on "Peacemakers" offers the first comprehensive engagement with the problems of peace in our age, through a meticulous and thorough study of the lives and thoughts of peacemakers of all ages.

OMAR KHAYYAM
On the Value of Time
Nick M. Loghmani

J. KRISHNAMURTI
Educator for Peace
Meenakshi Thapan

For more information about this series, please visit: www.routledge.com/Peacemakers/book-series/PCMK

J. KRISHNAMURTI

Educator for Peace

Meenakshi Thapan

LONDON AND NEW YORK

First published 2022
by Routledge
4 Park Square, Milton Park, Abingdon,
Oxon OX14 4RN

and by Routledge
605 Third Avenue, New York, NY 10158

Routledge is an imprint of the Taylor & Francis Group, an informa business

© 2022 Meenakshi Thapan

The right of Meenakshi Thapan to be identified as author of this work has been asserted in accordance with sections 77 and 78 of the Copyright, Designs and Patents Act 1988.

All rights reserved. No part of this book may be reprinted or reproduced or utilised in any form or by any electronic, mechanical, or other means, now known or hereafter invented, including photocopying and recording, or in any information storage or retrieval system, without permission in writing from the publishers.

Trademark notice: Product or corporate names may be trademarks or registered trademarks, and are used only for identification and explanation without intent to infringe.

British Library Cataloguing-in-Publication Data
A catalogue record for this book is available from the British Library

Library of Congress Cataloging-in-Publication Data
A catalog record for this book has been requested

ISBN: 978-1-032-02219-2 (hbk)
ISBN: 978-1-032-26970-2 (pbk)
ISBN: 978-1-003-29073-5 (ebk)

DOI: 10.4324/9781003290735

Typeset in Sabon
by Apex CoVantage, LLC

To the memory of our beloved mother
Aruna Thapan, *nee* Ahluwalia
(1931–2021)

CONTENTS

Foreword   *viii*
HIS HOLINESS, TENZIN GYATSO, THE 14TH DALAI LAMA

Series Editor's Preface   *ix*
Preface and Acknowledgements   *xi*

1 Introducing J. Krishnamurti   1

2 Krishnamurti's Educational Vision   14

3 Krishnamurti's Educational Challenge   27

4 The Practice of 'Right' Education: Rishi Valley Education Centre (RVEC)   68

5 Challenges and Continuities   87

References   *94*
Index   *102*

FOREWORD

THE DALAI LAMA

In this age of globalisation, we must recognise how deeply interconnected our lives have become. We can no longer emulate the ways of our forefathers, limiting our concerns to our own community or nation. Our sense of responsibility must include the wellbeing of all of humanity; we must develop universal responsibility.

Modern education emphasises the enrichment of our intellect; however, we also should include an understanding of how to achieve peace of mind. It is important that education should teach us how to live properly and how to balance our wish for physical comfort with mental peace.

Professor Meenakshi Thapan's book, *J. Krishnamurti: Educator for Peace*, addresses the views of Krishnamurti, particularly his belief that education must include the cultivation of humanity and goodness. I am sure readers will find this book both interesting and beneficial.

30 September 2021

SERIES EDITOR'S PREFACE

Peace is one of the central concepts of the spiritual and political life of humanity. When we study the world's religious and philosophical teachings, whether they are from the East or the West, we see that one of the basic ideals of all religions is peace. Peace does not imply simply the absence of war. It implies harmony, justice, and empathy. Empathy is the key to education of peace in our world. In other words, despite the vast differences of values between cultures and traditions, it is still possible to grasp an understanding of one another, by 'empathy'. Therefore, we can maintain that all cultures have a shared core of common humanity. Throughout centuries, peacemakers endorsed a 'shared human horizon' which, according to them, had the critical force of avoiding moral anarchy and relativism while acknowledging the plurality of modes of being human. As a matter of fact, the first step for peacemakers has always been not only to assume that there are differences among nations, cultures, and traditions of thought but also to admit that people may have different value systems which need to be understood and approached dialogically and critically. Philosophy of peace is, thus, expressed here in the idea of a 'self-respecting' community or nation which strives to remove its own imperfections instead of necessarily judging others. As a result, peacemaking is always a call not only to cultivate humility but also to foster pluralism. Such a view is essential if we are to avoid the danger of cultural conformity and move towards the recognition of shared values of humanity and the acceptance of what Martin Luther

SERIES EDITOR'S PREFACE

King, Jr. called the 'cosmic companionship'. Put it differently, we can say that it would be an error to hope that we can ever achieve a truly universal vision of peace without an intercultural approach to the idea of civilisation. Peacemakers have always been in favour of a farsighted peacemaking in our world, which has seriously advocated the logic of solidarity and civic friendship beyond national selfishness and global exclusion. Let us not forget that all peacemakers, either man or woman, young or old, from the West or the East, were all engaged in the process of peace-seeking by fighting for care, openness, and empathy as constructive forms of being together. Today in a different manner and in a changed tone, but with the same moral courage and dissenting voice, this series on 'Peacemakers' offers the first comprehensive engagement with the problems of peace in our age, through a meticulous and thorough study of the lives and thoughts of peacemakers of all ages.

Ramin Jahanbegloo

PREFACE AND ACKNOWLEDGEMENTS

Undoubtedly, J. Krishnamurti was an unusual teacher. Not only was he deeply concerned about the decay and disintegration of society around the world, he also sought to address this with a focus on bringing about change through self-inquiry. Every individual is responsible not just for her own life but for rest of humanity, and it is this sense of complete responsibility that he sought to inculcate through education in the schools started by him. This work aims to provide an understanding of Krishnamurti's views on the human predicament in a globally disintegrating world, marked by conflict, divisions, wars, and climate change as well as examine his educational thought and its potential for change. There is a special focus on Krishnamurti as an educator for peace and the school as the nucleus of his perception for psychological development and academic excellence. It is within an educational setting that Krishnamurti hopes the seeds for individual and social change will be planted and grow through a nurturing, affectionate, and enabling environment.

At the heart of Krishnamurti's concern for bringing about the 'good society' is his unerring faith in the potential and purpose of the human subject. The child, the individual, the human subject, in his view, is not merely a tabula rasa on which society writes itself; in fact, the capacity for change and renewal, at all levels of social life, through education, lies in the individual who can exercise judgement, restraint, as well as act from a consciousness that seeks to understand oneself in relation to others, and therefore act from that extended self. Agency is therefore central to Krishnamurti's understanding of the human subject and her or his role in society.

At the same time, there are challenges that are experienced by both educators and children. It is important to understand the dilemmas and difficulties in such schools where there are no precise instructions for the implementation of Krishnamurti's educational thought. Teachers and children work to circumvent the pressures and demands of social institutions through dialogue, engagement, negotiation, and debate. Acts of communication are central to relationship in such spaces, and this is one way through which the school culture seeks to dispel difficulties as well as creates an ethos where children may flourish. The work concludes with a reflection on how the Krishnamurti schools, the Rishi Valley Education Centre, in particular, have provided an impetus to Krishnamurti's ideas on education, the methods used, and the possibilities that are created for change at both individual and societal levels.

I thank His Holiness, Tenzin Gyatso, the 14th Dalai Lama, for taking time out of his busy schedule to write the foreword. Although Krishnamurti makes a complete departure from conventional thought, his work comes closest to Buddhism in its essential premise centred as it is in the interconnected nature of being and with self-inquiry in everyday life. It is also important that the Dalai Lama's emphasis today on an education that focuses on human goodness for the well-being of society has deep resonances with Krishnamurti's perspective on 'right' education. While at the University of Delhi, I had the privilege of organising several conferences and meetings on education, human consciousness, and universal ethics, at the Dalai Lama's initiative, with his support and active participation. I am deeply grateful to him for his generosity of time and attention that he gave to these meetings that were attended by many young people at the university and beyond. I would also like to express my profound sense of gratitude to Radhika and Hans Herzberger for a deep and lasting friendship and to Radhika and Dr. A. Kumaraswamy at Rishi Valley for their comments and suggestions which have strengthened this work. I am indebted to Santhi Narasimhan for her painstaking support in the finalisation of this manuscript and for her invaluable help in preparing the index.

This work is dedicated to the memory of my mother, Aruna Thapan, *nee* Ahluwalia, who, along with my father, introduced me to Shri J. Krishnamurti at Kitty Shiva Rao's home in Delhi in November 1973. I remain indebted to her for this, her steadfast love and unconditional support over the years. Passing away on 7 October 2021, she unfortunately did not live to hold this book in her hands.

Meenakshi Thapan
Rishi Valley
October 2021

1
INTRODUCING J. KRISHNAMURTI

J. Krishnamurti (1895–1986) was a radical teacher who was concerned with changing the world. He did not come upon this through adherence to a particular ideology or by taking the well-travelled path of pushing a political agenda for social transformation. He also did not have an instrumental approach to understanding education which he considered essential for change. Krishnamurti was instead concerned with the global crises that beset the world at the time he lived and which he knew would only escalate over time. He was certain that bemoaning violence or organising a revolution was not the answer:

> The tears of mankind have not washed away man's desire to kill. No religion has stopped war; all of them, on the contrary, have encouraged it, blessed the weapons of war; they have divided the people. Governments are isolated and cherish their insularity. The scientists are supported by governments. The preacher is lost in his words and images.
> (Krishnamurti 1987a: 62)

Peace, Krishnamurti argued,

> is not achieved through any ideology, it does not depend on legislation; it comes only when we as individuals begin to understand our own psychological process. If we avoid the responsibility of acting individually and

wait for some new system to establish peace, we shall merely become slaves of that system.

(Krishnamurti 2019a: 66)

It is on each one of us that the responsibility for the world and for peace and well-being of society depends.

In his view, it was education alone that could provide 'freedom' from the conditioning and the systems that perpetuate conflict, war, and violence. He warned, 'If you want things to be continued as they are then you must accept the present system which brings constant wars and confusion, never a moment of peace in the world' (Krishnamurti 2016: 14). However, 'to find reality there must be freedom, freedom from conditioned thinking, to discover if there is not something beyond the sensate values – not the absurd political freedom but freedom from conditioning, from the psychological demands that condition thought' (Krishnamurti 2016: 14). Krishnamurti envisaged that it is the right kind of education that would bring about this freedom and a form of human intelligence devoid of the burden of memory, tradition, and regurgitated knowledge, and that would in turn enable peace and allow a good society to flourish.[1]

Educator for Peace

The most significant aspect of Krishnamurti's views on education is his ability to identify the transformative potential of education, not merely as that which we usually understand as resulting in human development and economic growth but which can help human beings understand themselves and others, thereby transforming social life. This quality of being able to focus on the potential of human beings to inquire into themselves, to understand their feelings, their thoughts, their relationships, is a unique way of addressing the promise that education holds out to us. While this may be more commonplace in some schools around the world today, it was certainly not the case when Krishnamurti first started addressing these concerns in the 1930s and 1940s.

This work seeks to understand Krishnamurti as an educator for peace through his educational thought and practices in the Krishnamurti schools, especially at the Rishi Valley Education Centre located in rural Andhra Pradesh, southern India. Peace education as it is understood in contemporary times is concerned with issues as wide-ranging as conflict resolution, human rights, non-violence, disarmament, the environment, and what is often referred to as 'personal education for peace'.[2] Betty Reardon, who has made a dedicated effort to write about and argue for peace education, says peace education is significant in teaching both 'about' peace and 'for' peace (2000: 399). She also argues that there is 'negative' peace (the absence of war and armed conflict) and 'positive' peace (that transcends negative peace). The latter includes the positive implementation of social justice; not only are forms of violence, war, and aggression absent in the social order but also the full realisation of all forms of human rights are present. The presence of both negative and positive peace establishes what Reardon refers to as 'authentic' peace: she 'conceives authentic peace as the abolition of the war system and the establishment of global justice and a global civic community. Peace, so conceived, is therefore an ethical imperative, a fundamental human right' (Snauwaert 2014: xii). This view of peace sets an ethical requirement to understanding peace and implementing a 'transformational' peace education focusing on pedagogies of learning that emphasise 'moral/ethical' reflective inquiry and care, concern, and commitment for humanity (Snauwaert 2014: xiv). Reardon's work, widely acknowledged, has resonances with educational thought and is an essential part of educational pedagogy for both students and teachers in terms of establishing an ethos of peace in and through education.[3]

In the current context, where divisiveness, violence, and hatred seem to define human relations, Krishnamurti's work has enormous relevance and seeks to bring an awareness about our role and responsibility as social beings. Krishnamurti has raised significant questions about the state of the world, about our tendency to remain passive, conditioned, and in a state of overwhelming confusion about how we relate to the world. At the same time, we think that we can bring an end to war and establish peace through protests and other means. At a talk at the United Nations in 1985, Krishnamurti said,

> Peace requires a great deal of intelligence, not just demonstrations against a particular form of war, against a nuclear or atom bomb and so on. Those are the products of minds, brains that are entrenched in nationalism, in some particular form of belief, ideology. So they are supplying armaments – the powerful ones, whether it be Russia, America, or England or France – armaments to the rest of the world, and they also talk about peace, supplying at the same time armaments.
> (Krishnamurti 1985a)

The hypocrisy of nations in dealing with war is on display when they view themselves as separate entities, with distinct territorial boundaries, ideological aims, and also consider the supply of armaments to the world a legitimate exercise. Peace then, Krishnamurti argues, is not a real goal for them. He adds,

> You may be a woman, I may be a man, you may be tall, dark, short and so on, but inwardly, psychologically, which is far more important, we are the rest of mankind. You are the rest of mankind, and so if you kill another, if you are in conflict with another, you are destroying yourself . . . there can only be peace when mankind, when you and I, have no conflict in ourselves.
> (Krishnamurti 1985a)

This is an essential aspect of Krishnamurti's view: the fact that we are all interconnected, not defined by different nations, religions, terrains, and ideologies. It is the recognition of this sameness and the understanding that it brings in relationship that we can start to see the beginning of peace. Krishnamurti asserted that this understanding has to be felt as an imperative,

> Please understand this not intellectually or ideologically or as an hypothesis, but as an actuality, a burning

reality, that you psychologically are the rest of mankind. . . . When you realize this, not emotionally, not as an intellectual concept but as something actual, real, true, then you will not kill another human being; you will never kill another, either verbally or intellectually, ideologically or physically, because then you are killing yourself. . . . If you are concerned with global peace, not just your own little peace in the backyard, . . . if you are really concerned, as most serious people must be concerned, that you are the rest of humanity, that's a great responsibility.

(Krishnamurti 1985b)

It is this sense of oneness and responsibility that an education for peace must foster.

Krishnamurti's method, which he articulated through his talks and writings spread over many decades and geographical locations, delineates an unconditioned, reflective approach and emphasises self-inquiry. In this aspect, he differs from the work of Reardon and others who seek to bring about peace through focusing on the ending of war, conflict, and injustice through education. There are essential components for peace and children as well as young adults need to understand this through the right educational methods such as dialogue and 'queries' or questioning aspects of political, social, and cultural life, thereby challenging prevailing norms. At the same time, Krishnamurti urges us to focus on a holistic approach that is indicative of an integrated approach to education. Such an approach takes account of all aspects of a child's development and does not focus on one or two or another, to the exclusion of the other significant but invisible aspects of growing up. Everything is of significance, not least of all, the teacher herself. Her development is of paramount importance. The teacher or resource person cannot therefore 'teach' peace education. The teacher and the student are both partners in this process of self-inquiry and relationship that helps in understanding our own actions, feelings, attitudes, perceptions, and a whole range of experiences as they unfold in the educational process.

INTRODUCING J. KRISHNAMURTI

Krishnamurti's work is essential to understand the possibilities for change through an education that is geared towards understanding the psychological dimension of individual life through which the individual would find the capacity for the transformation of social life. Krishnamurti's concern with the decay of values in society that is increasingly built on the principle of profit and self-gain through the destruction of nature, widespread corruption, unfair means, and excessive violence, and concurrently, his deep faith in the vastness of human potential results in his insightful approach to education. He postulates an educational practice that first teaches young children about the value of life itself, and in that process, enables and nurtures an awareness and commitment to goals devoid of self-aggrandisement, and to the protection of that life including the world of nature, the less privileged and marginalised, and the transformation of society. The values that Krishnamurti highlights therefore are embedded in the worth of an individual and what she is able to make of her life. Radhika Herzberger, former Director of the Rishi Valley Education Centre, has spent several decades working out Krishnamurti's approach in practice and has noted,

> If there is a cornerstone to Krishnamurti's teachings, it is that one was really the master of one's life, one's destiny. . . . There is no refuge, neither in God nor in other human beings. . . . One is one's own refuge; one's own teacher and one's own disciple. That gives one both courage and a certain independence and no self-pity.
> (Herzberger, as cited in Blau 1995: 261)

This faith in the agency of the human subject and her capabilities for change sets Krishnamurti apart from other teachers and practitioners of peace and transformation. The first step lies with oneself and initiates the cascading effects for change.

Krishnamurti's Life

Krishnamurti had an extraordinary life spread out across the world in different homes, venues, and continents. He was born in 1895 in a small town, Madanapalle, in Chittoor district in

Andhra Pradesh. There are no distinguishing features of this dusty, busy city that it has now become except that the Besant Theosophical College located here was started by Annie Besant in 1915.[4] Krishnamurti's parents lived here, and he grew up with his siblings until he was almost 15 years old. It is said that he had a somewhat 'vacant' look about him and was hardly interested in anything much happening around him. His father was fascinated by Theosophy and moved to Madras on his retirement, to be closer to the Theosophical Society headquartered at Adyar. After this move, Krishnamurti's life trajectory was to change radically and permanently.[5]

Krishnamurti's early life is tied to the theosophical movement in India that started in the later years of the nineteenth century. The theosophical movement was founded by Madame Helena Blavatsky, a spiritual leader of Russian origin who lived during the second half of the nineteenth century. The movement was established as the Theosophical Society in New York in 1875. Blavatsky claimed to have a range of psychic powers including telepathy, clairvoyance, and travelling on the astral plane. In 1882, Blavatsky and her collaborator, Henry Steel Olcott travelled to Adyar, in modern-day Chennai, India, where they established their international headquarters. They found a larger audience in India than in Europe, primarily because Theosophy appealed to Asian religions. Both Blavatsky and Olcott officially converted to Buddhism and esoteric teachings based on 'the Kabala, Gnosticism, Meister Eckhart, Paracelsus, and later, Hindu, Buddhist and Tibetan beliefs such as karma and reincarnation' were the foundation of Theosophy (Chandmal 1985: 9).[6] In Adyar, they began publishing a journal called *The Theosophist* and gathered a large number of followers.

As early as 1889, Blavatsky was saying that the purpose of Theosophy was to prepare humanity for the coming of the Lord Maitreya, the World Teacher, in a new reincarnation. After Blavatsky's death, Annie Besant and C.W. Leadbeater considered it their task to carry on this work, part of which was the preparation of a disciple who would serve as a vehicle for the Teacher. It is Leadbeater who apparently 'found' Krishnamurti in 1909 while he was playing on the beach at Adyar, and discovered that his 'aura' did not contain an iota of selfishness (Chandmal 1985: 10).[7] In time, Annie Besant was to formally adopt the boy, announce his role as the 'World Teacher', provide him with an appropriate education and upbringing as well as with the organisation that would befit the stature of the World Teacher, and enable the unfolding of his 'teachings'.[8]

Krishnamurti was trained in the theosophical teachings that included the reading of esoteric texts, meditation, as well as astral travel on different planes, to communicate with 'the masters' and then, imbibing all this by writing it all down. It appears that Krishnamurti was in touch with one such master on the astral plane, Master Kuthumi, who lived somewhere in Tibet. He would visit the master at night and write down his teachings in the morning (Chandmal 1985: 10). This was subsequently published as a small book *At the Feet of the Master* in 1910 and has been translated into more than 30 languages. In addition, Krishnamurti received conventional education with lessons in different subjects, especially the English language and Western behaviour. It was a lot of hard work, and Krishnamurti succumbed to it under the tutelage of Leadbeater, a prominent Theosophist who, as mentioned earlier, 'discovered' Krishnamurti and had been in charge of him ever since.[9] In 1922, Krishnamurti was at Ojai and underwent what is referred to as 'the process' by those who know him. This was an inexplicable physical and psychological process that shook him and those who happened to be with him, notably his brother, Nitya, to whom he was very close. The latter has described the entire process that lasted a few days in a letter he wrote to Annie Besant.[10] It was a most unusual process that changed Krishnamurti's life completely. He experienced physical discomfort and pain at the nape of his neck and throughout his body as well as experiencing a separation from his physical body. At the end of it all, Krishnamurti notes,

> There was such profound calmness both in the air and within myself, the calmness of the bottom of a deep unfathomable lake. Like the lake, I felt my physical body, with its mind and emotions, could be ruffled on the surface but nothing, nay nothing, could disturb the

> calmness of my soul. . . . I was supremely happy. . . . Nothing could ever be the same. I have drunk at the clear and pure waters at the source of the fountain of life and my thirst was appeased. . . . I have touched compassion which heals all sorrow and suffering; it is not for myself, but for the world.
>
> (Krishnamurti, as cited in Blau 1995: 34)[11]

Apart from this life-changing experience that continued off and on in Krishnamurti's life, his brother Nitya died of tuberculosis in 1925, while Krishnamurti was at sea, travelling to India. It was a very sharp blow to him as he had been made to believe by the Theosophists and all their esoteric rituals that his brother would somehow triumph his illness and live. He wrote in 1926, 'a new strength, born of suffering, is pulsating in the veins and a new sympathy and understanding is being born of past suffering' (Krishnamurti, as cited in Blau 1995: 38). He now began to question Theosophy's occult beliefs and rituals and to shake off the view that he was to become the new 'world teacher', coming to save the world.

Krishnamurti survived the Theosophists' undertaking to make him a 'messiah', 'educate', and civilise him but, by 1929, he had tired of the whole enterprise.[12] In a powerful speech, he dissolved the Order of the Star, an organisation with more than 60,000 members. He resigned from the Theosophical Society and from every other organisation he was associated with. In his speech, he emphasised the fundamental premise of religion as that which could not be organised:

> I maintain that Truth is a pathless land, and you cannot approach it by any path whatsoever, by any religion, by any sect. That is my point of view, and I adhere to that absolutely and unconditionally. Truth, being limitless, unconditioned, unapproachable by any path whatsoever, cannot be organized; nor should any organization be formed to lead or to coerce people along any particular path.
>
> (Krishnamurti 1929)

The Theosophical Society and all that it stood for had been grooming him as the coming 'World Teacher' and by this act, Krishnamurti severed all his links with the organisation in the presence of Dr. Annie Besant who was in the audience. He stated that his only goal was 'to make man free, to urge him towards freedom, to help him to break away from all limitations, for that alone will give him eternal happiness' (Krishnamurti 1929). Having been imprisoned in a sense by the theosophists all his life until now, Krishnamurti was eager to not only break free but also assert his own perspective that was to be remarkably different from that of Theosophy.

No doubt, Krishnamurti had a privileged upbringing after the first 14 years of his life which he spent in nondescript, dusty towns in Andhra Pradesh. He was groomed to be the 'World Teacher' by the Theosophical Society that laid out all the infrastructure, vast tracts of property, and an organisational structure at his disposal. Krishnamurti turned all this down and sought independence from an organisation that was stifling him, making him fit into a pattern and regurgitate the 'truths' it sought to propagate. He rejected all this and more when, in 1929, he cut his ties with the Order of the Star, an organisation Besant had established for the 'Second Coming'. This was not, however, a 'political action'. It was in fact an act that was devoid of all politics, of all posturing, ideological moorings, or any kind of gimmickry. It was an action that was borne out of deep conviction, subsequent to the passing of his young brother, that no organisation, religious or otherwise, could provide the key to understanding yourself. After this, Krishnamurti spent the rest of his life speaking around the world to large audiences about the possibilities of breaking free from the shackles of the mind through self-inquiry, understanding oneself in relationship, and having an open spirit to the rest of humanity. He also engaged in dialogue, on these themes and others, with scientists notably the physicist David Bohm (Krishnamurti and Bohm 1985; Peat 1996; Moody 2017), philosophers, psychologists, and others over the globe. The philosopher Aldous Huxley was a friend who encouraged Krishnamurti to publish his writings and in fact wrote the foreword to Krishnamurti's book, *The First and Last Freedom* (1954). After listening to a talk by Krishnamurti, Huxley is believed to have said, 'It was like listening to a sermon of the Buddha' (as cited in Moody 2017: 34). The Anglo-Irish playwright George Bernard Shaw admired Krishnamurti and when the broadcast of Shaw's play *Androcles and the Lion*, and Krishnamurti's talks were banned at the same time in New Zealand in 1934, he said,

> A far less excusable case is the refusal to allow Mr Krishnamurti to broadcast. He is a religious teacher of the greatest distinction, who is listened to with profit and assent by members of all churches and sects, and the prohibition is an ignorant mistake.
> (Shaw, as cited in Blau 1995: 105)

Over the years, Krishnamurti's talks and writings have been published and translated into many languages. Foundations to run his schools and publish and disseminate his thought and work were established in India, the United Kingdom, and the United States. Krishnamurti himself continued to ceaselessly meet large audiences globally and talk about 'freedom' in approaching 'truth' and in the significance of the present, the 'what is', rather than that of thought, memory, and all aspects of conditioning that so limit our ability to 'see'. Peace, he argued, lies in self-understanding and in 'right' relationship with nature, ideas, and fellow human beings. It was an emphasis on the everyday, the ordinary life, in relationship to others, that Krishnamurti highlighted. At the same time, he was concerned about the social and psychological conditioning that has ensnared us in its grip due to which we have habituated ways of acting, thinking, and being. Change is important, to break out of this conditioning. It is significant that at the heart of Krishnamurti's perspective on change, there is an overwhelming accent on 'right' education for bringing up new generations of integrated human beings who would transform the world.

Notes

1 Krishnamurti used 'freedom' in a particular sense, not as the ability to do whatever one wants or likes to do. I will examine this aspect of his thought later in this work.
2 Personal education for peace includes 'strategies such as meditation and visualisation, relaxation, yoga, tai chi, artwork, song and dance, story-telling, affirmation use, emotional literacy, self-esteem building, cooperative games, and inclusion activities' (https://peace learner.org/about-2/what-do-peace-educators-teach-about-content/, accessed on 15 May, 2021).
3 For further understanding Reardon's perspective and vision about pedagogies for peace education, see Reardon (1988, 2000, 2001), Snauwaert (2019). Krishna Kumar (2016) has pointed out the lacuna in peace education in schools in India and the urgent need to redress this; for a practical guide on peace education, see, for example, Romano and Simms (2012).
4 Starting out as first Woods National College, the Besant Theosophical College was first affiliated to Madras University but later moved to Visva-Bharati University, Santiniketan, as it became associated with Annie Besant's 'nationalist' activities for 'home rule'. Rabindranath Tagore visited the College in 1919 and translated the national anthem which he had earlier written into English during his time here. The College is now affiliated with Sri Venkateshwara University at Tirupathi, Andhra Pradesh.
5 Lutyens has written Krishnamurti's biography in three parts (Lutyens 1975, 1983, 1988); Williams (2004) provides a detailed and nuanced account about Krishnamurti's extraordinary life.
6 To understand the workings of Theosophy as a religion, see Blavatsky (1962, 1972, 1987).
7 Krishnamurti's father had retired from his position in Madanapalle and moved to Adyar in January 1909 to live close to the Theosophical Society of which he was a member and educate his four sons.
8 See Jayakar (1987) for a powerful rendering of Krishnamurti's teachings and of her life intertwined with Krishnamurti's; see also Lutyens (1975).
9 Krishnamurti was not successful at conventional educational certification and failed all the examinations he ever took (Chandmal 1985; Blau 1995; Williams 2004).
10 See Blau (1995: 32–33) for detailed extracts from Nitya's letter.
11 Jayakar describes it as the awakening of 'the *kundalini* energy principle' (1987: 47). See Jayakar (1987: 46 ff). More recently, Lee (2020) has attempted an analysis of 'the process' that continued from 1922 until Krishnamurti's death in 1986.

12 It is said that the death of Krishnamurti's brother, Nitya, despite having been told by his teachers that he would not be 'allowed' to die, was an important factor in his disillusionment with the training he had received. Chandmal writes, 'He was never to depend on anything or be attached to anyone again, and this became a central theme in his teachings' (1985: 11).

2
KRISHNAMURTI'S EDUCATIONAL VISION

At the outset, it is important to state that Krishnamurti's educational vision was far from an utopian idea wrapped up in an idealistic presentation of education for a 'good' child or a virtuous society. Krishnamurti has time and time again asserted the need for the transformation of society for which a new mind is necessary, a new imagination for constructing oneself in relation to the world. This is not in some kind of a romantic idealisation of the relationship between the individual and society, but by emphasising the responsibility of individuals to society and to the earth, Krishnamurti hoped to work on 'relationship' as critical to the process of education. Both the child or the student and the teacher are active agents in Krishnamurti's construction, fully capable of bringing about this change through engagement with others, with society, ideas, and nature. Hierarchy and inequality do not necessarily determine social relations in education, and therefore social and cultural reproduction through education is not inevitable. Contra Althusser (1971), Bourdieu and Passeron (1977), and other writings on social reproduction through education, Krishnamurti's educational perspective may be seen as viewing the human subject as one imbued with 'agency' and 'moral' value, who is being educated as a 'social' being, fully engaged in the twin processes of self-inquiry and social transformation.

Krishnamurti's view further suggests that students and teachers are not cowed down by society, the reproductive aspects of educational practice, or the overwhelming preponderance of class, caste, or religious divisions that inhere in society. In fact, they seek to engage first, with a process of understanding themselves, in relationship to society, with all its cleavages, anxieties, dilemmas, and through that, work in transformative ways to change society. This view presents the idea of the cultural 'production' of the educated person. In their insightful work, Levinson and Holland argue, 'For while the educated person is culturally *produced* in definite sites, the educated person also culturally *produces* cultural forms' (Levinson and Holland 1996: 14, emphasis in the original). They take this further to argue that it is not just the school where this production takes place but may be extended to spaces outside school: 'This creative practice generates understandings and strategies which may in fact move well beyond the school, transforming aspirations, household relations, local knowledges, and structures of power' (Levinson and Holland 1996: 14). Society in its entirety is our making, and not created by 'some gods in heaven', as Krishnamurti often said. Krishnamurti's effort was to bring about an awareness in his audiences, public talks, and schools, of this significant understanding: responsibility for the earth and society inheres in each one of us and it is this sense of responsibility that needs to be awakened and nurtured.

> A human being psychologically is the whole of mankind. He not only represents it but he is the whole of the human species. He is essentially the whole psyche of mankind. On this actuality various cultures have imposed the illusion that each human being is different.... As the representative of the whole human race, your response is whole not particular. So responsibility has a totally different meaning. One has to learn the art of this responsibility. If one grasps the full significance that one is psychologically the world, then responsibility becomes overpowering love.
> (Krishnamurti, 15 November 1978)

For Krishnamurti, it was important that educators do not merely teach academic subjects at school but cultivate in children, their total responsibility to the rest of humankind, the earth, and nature. Krishnamurti was quite clear that this could be brought about through an engagement with children at school. Krishnamurti's focus on education as the *sine qua non* for processes leading to a just social world, free from violence, fear, and sorrow, was based on his acute understanding of the twin processes of the agency of the human agent and possibilities for change through an integrated educational process.

In Krishnamurti's words,

> 'School' comes from the Greek word for leisure – leisure in which to learn, a place where students and teachers can flower, a place where a future generation can be prepared, because schools are meant for that, not just merely to turn out human beings as mechanical, technological instruments – . . . but also flower as human beings, without fear, without confusion, with great integrity.
>
> (Krishnamurti 2019b: 87)

The school, and the children, teachers, and others in it, is central to Krishnamurti's perception about how to begin to work for social transformation.

The Krishnamurti Foundation India (KFI) runs six schools, and there is also one school each in the United Kingdom and the United States. The schools are co-educational and mostly residential. The oldest school is located at Rishi Valley in rural Andhra Pradesh. It was Krishnamurti's first school and has been around for about 90 years. Rajghat Besant School, which is over 80 years old, is located on the banks of the Ganges in Varanasi. Started by Annie Besant, Vasanta College, an old and well-established women's college for undergraduate and graduate studies in various disciplines (affiliated to the Benares Hindu University), functions under the aegis of the Krishnamurti Foundation India, also in Varanasi. The School KFI is a day school, in Madras (now, Chennai). It began in 1973 at Poes Garden and moved to Damodar Gardens of the Theosophical Society in 1979. It has very recently moved to Thazambhur, just outside Chennai. The

Valley School in Bengaluru, a day-boarding school, was established in 1978 and is located in a quieter part of the city. Sahyadri School located near Pune is situated on Tiwai Hill in the midst of the Sahyadri range in Maharashtra. All these are small schools, as compared to other residential schools in the country, with an average of 300–350 students each. The most recent KFI school, Pathashaala in Kanchipuram district, Tamil Nadu, set up in 2010, has a smaller student population and is slowly growing. The campus uses energy sparingly and is designed with solar energy and a windmill. A unique feature of the school is its design as a zero-blackwater campus by the use of dry composting toilets.

In addition, there are some outreach programmes associated with the education and health centres that have been engaged in pioneering pedagogic and other work for rural communities. These are located at Rishi Valley in rural Andhra Pradesh, Rajghat, at Varanasi, Sahyadri, near Pune, Pathashaala, near Elimichampet in Tamil Nadu, and the Kaigal Education and Environment Programme (part of the Bangalore Centre).[1] Apart from the headquarters of the KFI in Vasanta Vihar, Chennai, Krishnamurti Study centres are located at all the schools and also in cities such as Mumbai and Kolkata and in Indore and Cuttack as well. These host video talks, discussions, and webinars on Krishnamurti on a regular basis. The KFI also has retreat centres in the Himalayas at Uttarkashi and Jalna in the Kumaon region. These are places where visitors can engage with Krishnamurti's work and spend time in quiet reflection and solitude.

On Education

Krishnamurti's own educational experience was remarkably inadequate and fraught with misery for the young Krishnamurti. Mark Lee tells us,

> Schooling for Krishnamurti must have been a classic, colonial nightmare rivalling a Dickensian novel, with strict Brahmin schoolmasters, corporal punishment,

and foreign textbooks. The Mylapore Grammar School in Madras where we first know of him attending classes forced him to study English, geography, and mathematics. Each of his textbooks is identified with his neat, printed, careful signature, but the learning environment was brutal and coercive. He was so passive a learner that when disciplined by the schoolmaster and told to wait outside the classroom, he did so well into the night, not having the sense to return to his house at the end of the day.

(Lee 2019: 129)

Elsewhere, a biographer notes that in Madras in 1909, Krishnamurti was 'having a bad time at school because he did not pay attention to what his teacher said. He was bullied and beaten to such an extent that it seemed he might fade away from life' (Williams 2004: 19). His misadventures in school and his tryst with education as he knew it then were perhaps to influence his own views on education and schooling. Later, when he was under the tutelage of the Theosophists, while he learnt English and French, and other subjects with private tutors, he was unable to pass a single examination and could not gain entrance into a university.

Education in fact occupied Krishnamurti's intent for almost his entire life, as he was speaking to the world about global crises and the ending of sorrow. The Theosophists, particularly Annie Besant, with her keen interest in education must have been an influence as evidenced in this early text, titled *Education as Service* (Krishnamurti 1912). It is said to have been written by someone else, perhaps to whom he was close at the time, in which he shares his own memories of his schooling experience, and wants to 'help others towards the right way of teaching' (1912).[2] The small book is all about the role of the teacher that is examined through different themes such as love, discrimination, good conduct, and so on. It is written during the time Krishnamurti was associated with the Theosophists, and his independent views had not yet taken root. Nonetheless, it foregrounds his early interest in the field of education that remained his life's work over the decades he spent talking and writing about it.

At the same time, Krishnamurti's visits to other educational institutions also affected his perceptions of what such institutions can do if they have the right vision and calibre. Krishnamurti visited the University of California in Berkeley in 1922 and deeply 'struck by the beauty of the place, the openness of the students, and the sense of equality he perceived in the community, he resolved to start an academic institution in India' (Herzberger n.d.a). He started two schools to begin with, one in Rishi Valley in southern India, and the Rajghat Besant School, just outside Benares (now, Varanasi) in northern India. At these schools, Krishnamurti hoped to set up first-rate educational institutions that would be concerned about learning in the sense he understood it to be, working with children as integrated human beings receiving a holistic, not fragmented, education.

Most educational institutions have taken on the role of merely imparting skills and knowledge in different academic subjects over a period of time to various age cohorts that pass through them. Krishnamurti set up schools where, apart from the paying attention to the pedagogic processes and activities associated with certification, there is a simultaneous effort among both students and teachers to engage with their emotions, behaviour, attitudes, and perceptions as well as understand the possibilities for agency in the public domain.

To ensure peace and harmony on the planet, which is a vast, hugely diverse and complex network of relationships among humans, nature, and the earth, one of the aims of the Krishnamurti schools is to ensure that students develop a global outlook. To this end, there is an attempt to not only enrich the curriculum with local knowledge and contexts but also bring about a deeper understanding of the fragile ecosystem and a consciousness about change at a global level. The idea of translocation is central to this analysis as it is the coming together of the local and the global, the earth and humanity, the individual and the collective, for developing greater consciousness about the fragility of the ecosystem and our attitude towards it. I use the term 'translocation' to emphasise the transcending of local or national boundaries, individual selves, and self-centred attitudes and goals. It also implies the opening out of the self towards humanity in a very diverse, global sense. It is translocation and its outcome, the opening out of the self, which will help us contend with divisiveness in society and the anxieties and vulnerabilities this gives rise to, thereby enabling the possibilities for peace.

It is possible to translate such a perspective to the cultural context of a school. Since Krishnamurti held that the transcendent is to be discovered through relentless questioning and choiceless observation, without justifying or condemning, the boundary between the transcendent and the worldly is not impermeable. There is a fluidity and openness through which we need to comprehend our relationships with others, not merely through a rational understanding but with our emotions and senses as well to enable the experience of interconnectedness. The ability to realise a child's 'goodness' does not rest on young children alone, with some help from an educator, as classical educational thought tells us.[3] Significantly, it rests on the ability of schools and teachers to provide an ethos, a culture, wherein cognition and emotion are both equally valued and nurtured so as to enable the development of a morality that is not steeped in religious diktats, nationalism, or petty virtue but rests on a sense of the 'moral worth' of individuals. To put Krishnamurti's educational thought in a nutshell, school cultures must enable the development of a secular morality that engenders empathy, compassion, and humanism. This will lead to a just equitable society that enshrines the values of peace and harmony on the planet.

Rabindranath Tagore (1861–1941) also argued for an education based on humanistic values that would contribute to building a more humane society, open to diversity and freedom of different kinds. This is the basis on which a civilisation could be built.

> I was brought up in an atmosphere of aspiration, aspiration for the expansion of the human spirit. We in our home sought freedom of power in our language, freedom of imagination in our literature, freedom of soul in our

religious creeds and that of mind in our social environment. Such an opportunity has given me confidence in the power of education which is one with life and only which can give us real freedom, the highest that is claimed for man, his freedom of moral communion in the human world. . . . I try to assert in my words and works that education has its only meaning and object in freedom.
(Tagore 1929: 73–74)

The emphasis on freedom did not imply an unrestrained freedom at Tagore's school (*Patha* Bhavan at Santiniketan) or that a certain kind of wilfulness was acceptable in thought and behaviour among students. Amartya Sen has recently noted of his time as a student at Santiniketan, 'the idea that the exercise of freedom has to be developed alongside the capacity to reason became increasingly clear to me as my education at Santiniketan proceeded. If you have freedom, you will have reason to exercise it' (Sen 2021: 42). Freedom in itself, as Krishnamurti has argued, is therefore of not much value as it does not foster a sense of responsibility and may lead to confusion and chaos. For Tagore, it included 'training to make use of the freedom to reason', and this 'exceptional combination' (Sen 2021: 42) emphasises the significance of freedom in educational practice.

Like Krishnamurti, Tagore believed that education in schools does not teach children anything apart from subject-based knowledge that does not adequately help children connect to nature or to the world.

From our very childhood habits are formed and knowledge is imparted in such a manner that our life is weaned away from nature and our mind and the world are set in opposition from the beginning of our days. Thus the greatest of educations for which we came prepared is neglected, and we are made to lose our world to find a bagful of information instead. We rob the child of his earth to teach him geography, of language to teach him grammar.
(Tagore 1917: 116–117)

Contrarily, Tagore sought to have a different kind of curriculum at Santiniketan, 'Rather than studying national cultures for the wars won and cultural dominance imposed, he advocated a teaching system that analysed history and culture for the progress that had been made in breaking down social and religious barriers' (O'Connell 2003). This laid the ground for developing and nurturing a global outlook among children and young adults. Tagore considered the values of humanism, freedom, and concern for others and the earth, central to an alternative form of education on the basis of which he founded Santiniketan in West Bengal between 1862 and 1888.[4]

Among other stalwarts, Sri Aurobindo (1872–1950), a nationalist and teacher, was concerned about the development of a form of 'integral' education, an 'education of the whole person' (Partho 2007: 19). The philosophy of integral education includes a process of 'self-knowledge, awakening of the true centre of one's being, and a consequent process of integration and harmony' (Partho 2007: 24). This method consists of an effort to understand and analyse one's psychological movements on the part of both the teacher and the child. Through such an understanding, there is a 'consciousness of the unity and harmony within oneself' and finally an awakening to the 'true centre of being' (Partho 2007: 27). Such a practice would necessarily entail a form of education that too is 'integral' in vision and practice and is focused on bringing about harmony and balance in the individual and society (Partho 2007: 221). It is assumed that such an education will bring about learning both from one's own psychological processes and from daily life, and therefore there will be harmony and balance between the individual and society. Peace as a consequence of the good society will no doubt be achieved as a result of this poise and stability. At the same time, Aurobindo was a nationalist and sought to develop a truly 'national' education that would not 'ignore modern truth and knowledge, but to take our foundation on our own being, our own mind, our own spirit' (Aurobindo, as cited in Sibia 2006: 7). 'Our own' presumably refers to an 'Indian' sociocultural reality as opposed to a Western language and civilisation that was being furthered by colonialist interests at the time. Nonetheless, Aurobindo and his followers firmly pursued the larger goal of a more holistic education for inner balance and a good life.[5] Krishnamurti, however, disavowed nationalism as a narrow cause that did not foster a global spirit and resulted in creating further schisms in societies that are heterogeneous and already overwhelmed by divisions.

In his pursuit of the good society, Krishnamurti emphasised the individual's relationship to society as well as to her responsibility for establishing such a society: 'You are the repository of all humanity. You are the world and the world is you. And, if there is a radical transformation in the very structure of the individual's psyche, it will affect the whole consciousness of man' (Krishnamurti 1993: 133–134). Krishnamurti's emphasis on 'goodness' as the foundation of a new society underlies his plea for a society devoid of any kinds of contradictions or dichotomies. A society without 'national economic divisions' underscores his obvious concern for the ending of economic and social inequalities. However, Krishnamurti emphasised that none of this can come about without an inner renewal or change and education is therefore the foundation on which the good society will build itself.

The good society is characterised as the democratic society in the language of philosophy today. Martha Nussbaum has argued that the values for a democratic society include 'the capacity for Socratic self-criticism and critical thought about one's own traditions . . . ability to see oneself as a member of a heterogeneous nation . . . and [the ability of] narrative imagination' (Nussbaum 2015: 69). These are to be cultivated in children and young people in primary and secondary schools and are at the basis of the 'cultivation of sympathy', a necessary ingredient in contemporary times. In fact, 'imaginative sympathy' is at the heart of good citizenship and can be made 'precise' in children through education (Nussbaum 2015: 71). The pursuit of compassion and altruism appears as a constant in the work of philosophers and educationists who argue for an educational model that nurtures the psychological dimensions of a student's education to be a responsible member of society in contemporary times. At the heart of their concern for bringing about the 'good society' is the unerring faith of these thinkers in the potential and purpose of the human subject. The child, the individual, the human subject, in their view, is not merely an empty slate on which society writes itself; indeed, the capacity for change and renewal, at all levels of social life, through education, lies in the individual who can exercise judgement, restraint, as well as act from a consciousness that seeks to contain conflict and discord and work for the benefit of others.

As early as 1909, M.K. Gandhi wrote in *Hind Swaraj* (1997) about an educational process that emphasises the domain of inner inquiry and integrity in creating a society that is embedded in ethics and values. Education is only a secondary state or process. First, the individual must have a strong foundation of moral principles on which education may rest 'as an ornament'. In other words, education, an external process involving institutions, techniques, and forms of knowledge, must be embedded in a strong ethical foundation that forms the base of all knowledge. Gandhi emphasised character building and ethics as the 'firm foundation' on which education rests. An education that is about 'knowledge and letters' alone is not going to fulfil an individual or bring happiness. Education has to be grounded in religion but not any specific religion with its rabid leaders mouthing hatred and violence. It is an ethics that is born from the religious attitude, but not grounded in any particular religion, that Gandhi seeks to emphasise in his quest for a secular morality as laying the ethical foundations of education. For him, it was important that religion was restored to its important place, having been eroded by the effects of Western civilisation.

Gandhi was focused in his critical assessment of the damage that the English language is doing to education in India and to the outcome of the blind faith of the Indian elite in the use of this language for Indian society at large. The 'disease of civilization' has enraptured us, Gandhi would say, and is the cause of the obsession with not only the English language but also the life of the intellect at the cost of moral sentiments. It is to counter such a fixation for things of the mind that in turn results in the denial of the dignity of manual labour that Gandhi emphasised the significance of physical work and crafts-based education as being essential to his definition of basic education in India.[6]

In the context of education in contemporary India, Gandhi's views are a vital commentary on the colonialist enterprise in education. Gandhi spent his lifetime not only fighting the political forms of colonialism and its presence in society but also for eradicating the enduring forms of colonialism through his emphasis on craft-based education, a language policy that sought to do away with English, and other initiatives. The extent to which he was successful is too well known to bear repetition. Our quest for industrialisation and 'modernisation', to keep us at par with the rest of the world, has resulted in the system of education that is in current practice. It is undoubtedly one that in its emphasis on science and technology, on the persistent prevalence of the English language and the elitism associated with qualifications and worldly success, has failed Gandhi completely. The idiom of Gandhi's critique rests on the idea of 'enslavement' to not only a language but also an entire way of thinking and acting that has been bequeathed to India by Macaulay's policy for education in India.[7]

Krishnamurti's vision is very different as he did not view nationalism as did Gandhi whose views about education were grounded in his anti-colonial position and perhaps was a political stance (Herzberger 2015: 108–109). At the same time, this does not mean that Gandhi was not rooted in tradition, culture, and religion. His faith in the path of *ahimsa* and religion as the foundation of all morality were deeply vested in what he considered as an authentic Indian past. Krishnamurti, however, was not embedded in any particular tradition, religion, or nationalistic perspective and viewed himself as a global citizen. As Herzberger notes, 'Krishnamurti traced the "disease" of nationalism to a syndrome that includes the construction of various "walls" in a drive for security, protection and ultimately for power' (Herzberger 2015: 110). Viewed thus, nationalism did not pave the way for peace and in fact, brought forth emotions that valorised a strong sense of self-identification, excessive patriotism, often resulting in conflict and violence. Krishnamurti as an educator for peace and his schools in India have had to contend with a colonial legacy that did not exactly pave an easy path for the implementation of his vision.

Notes

1 For more details on all these institutions, please see www.kfionline.org/education-centres/ as well as the individual websites of the different entities.
2 It is well known that this book was perhaps not written by Krishnamurti himself but by his teachers in the Theosophical Society at the time.
3 See, for example, Locke (1692), Rousseau (1974).
4 At first, Tagore set up an ashram at Santiniketan. In 1901, he set up a school *Patha* Bhavan, the well-known Visva-Bharati University was established in 1919 and an Institute for Rural Reconstruction in 1922, at Santiniketan.
5 Aurobindo established the Aurobindo Ashram in Puducherry in Tamil Nadu, India, and the Ashram Trust runs a school and a college for undergraduate studies, based on these principles. Auroville, also based on the thought of Sri Aurobindo and The Mother (his foremost disciple), was established in 1968 and runs different kinds of educational and other institutions.
6 For more on Gandhi's educational thought, see Gandhi (1909); and for an insightful understanding, see Kumar (1997).
7 For the infamous Macaulay's Minute on Education in India (1835), see www.columbia.edu/itc/mealac/pritchett/00generallinks/macaulay/txt_minute_education_1835.html (accessed on 2 September, 2021).

3
KRISHNAMURTI'S EDUCATIONAL CHALLENGE

The educational landscape in India and the kinds of historical and social challenges to Krishnamurti's educational vision need to be understood in order to appreciate the challenges that are faced by his schools. Undoubtedly, educational settings in India are dominated in part by the history of the educational ideal of the colonial citizen (Kumar 1991). The colonial citizen has been produced and reproduced through the advent of 'modern' education in the late eighteenth and nineteenth centuries that emphasised a particular frame that sought to perfect the individual through moral education (provided by the missionaries) and civic education (exalted, prescribed, and perpetuated by the colonisers). The aim itself was suspect: to civilise the native and to replace indigenous knowledge with 'modern' forms of knowledge and ways of accessing it. The objective was to erode and ultimately eliminate indigenous culture and replace it with an alien institution that had very little to do with the lives and culture of the colonised. Such a view was undoubtedly instrumental in its aim to further colonial ideals at the cost of indigenous perspectives. The well-known Gandhian and historian of education, Dharampal notes, 'the neglect and deliberate uprooting of Indian education, the measures that were employed to this end, and its replacement by an alien and rootless system . . . had several consequences for India' (2000: 86). Among these was an 'obliteration of literacy and knowledge' of such enormous dimensions that India has subsequently been unable to make a significant dent in its manifestation.

It also resulted in producing citizens who defined themselves in terms of the education they received, as first and foremost, a representative of 'another' culture and civilisation. It has, moreover, kept 'most educated Indians ignorant of the society they live in, the culture that sustains this society and their fellow beings' (Dharampal 2000: 86). In a sense, it destroyed what Dharampal refers to as the 'Indian social balance' (Dharampal 2000: 86). In other words, the British were really after a 'cultural conquest': 'the primary purpose was to build a cultural dependency among the educated and the ruling classes so that revolutionary overthrow would never be a likely alternative' (Carnoy 1974: 100). This form of education, whatever its goals, brought Indian education into a wider social and linguistic setting and simultaneously brought about a form of inequality that persists: the elite constituted by the English-speaking, educated 'modern' human subject and the large mass of Indians educated in the vernacular in subjects that often do not connect to their everyday existence, an abysmal quality of educational tools and pedagogic practices and almost no infrastructure.[1]

This is only one aspect of the educational legacy inherited by India. Education has always been concerned with the human subject and with the processes of socialisation that underlie all schooling to develop, shape, and mould this subject in one way or another. The implications of this are far-reaching and have consequences for the growth and development not only of individuals but also for the well-being of society as a whole. Education as socialisation is actually about how the 'self' is constituted in relation to the world, and how school reproduces society through the organisation and content of the curriculum and through discursive modes of interaction and communication. This central motif of the idea of education is commonly understood but rarely articulated: the processes in educational practice that result in the constitution of the self. There are manifold practices at work within the space of the school, the peer group, and the community that are all engaged in the process of constructing the self. The school therefore is a hub for not only different kinds of activity but also a space where relationships of different kinds are constructed, constituted, maintained, contested, or celebrated. There is first a relationship to knowledge;

to the written text; to ideas and their limits; to peers, teachers, and other school personnel; and to the entire assemblage of activities, events, and emotions that constitute the daily life of the school. The individual self is constituted therefore always in relation to the social; this does not happen only as an arbitrary imposition or inculcation; it is always a simultaneous creation and engagement although constrained by the limiting and restraining aspects of such an engagement.

School education in India is also fraught with many difficulties of access to schools by all children regardless of caste, religion, or gender, their retention, availability, and quality of teachers, among other factors. However, children belonging to specific castes, gender, adivasi or religious communities often face particular difficulties. Krishnamurti was concerned about these aspects of educational practice and sought to provide education to the communities in which the Krishnamurti schools are established. His work is fundamentally focused on an oft-neglected aspect of educational work, the integrated development of the child. He decried the focus on the cognitive and technological aspects of education alone. He was certain that 'right' education must be centred on the whole child, all aspects of a child's existence and not merely a single aspect with a denial or neglect of all others. The freedom of the human subject, as Krishnamurti defined it, is not something to be acquired or grasped from others but comes with an understanding of oneself in inquiry in and through relationship. Freedom, as Krishnamurti argued, cannot come from someone else:

> . . . you cannot depend on others, you cannot expect someone to give you freedom and order. . . . So, you have to find out how to bring about order in yourself. That is, you have to watch and find out for yourself what it means to bring about virtue in yourself. . . . Virtue is order. So, you have to find out in yourself how to be good, how to be kind, how to be considerate. And out of that consideration, out of that watching, you bring about order and therefore freedom.
>
> (Krishnamurti 2018a: 32)

The process of self-inquiry is critical to this endeavour of watching oneself, observing one's reactions, seeing how one conducts oneself, in relationship with others, nature, ideas, and objects.

Identities, Violence, and Conflict

One of Krishnamurti's greatest concerns was to help us understand the dangers of 'identification with' an idea, a cause, a belief, a religion, and so on. The deepest sense of identification is with one's self. Krishnamurti points out, 'Now, what is "myself", and what is it to be identified with myself? Is there a myself or is the myself a series of words, images, which thought has put together, calling it "myself"? And with that I want to identify' (Krishnamurti Saanen 1973, as cited in Krishnamurti 2019c: 13–14). At another time, Krishnamurti was asked whether there is a 'real' self, apart from the 'me'. He says,

> You all, I am sure, feel there is something else beyond this 'me', which has been called the higher self, the sublime or the supreme self. The moment we use the word 'self', or use any word to describe that which is beyond the self, the 'me', it is still the self.
> (Krishnamurti, Brockwood Park, 28 August 1979, as cited in Krishnamurti 2019c: 25)

So, the self, and attachment to the self, through identification with the self, is the problem and, taking Krishnamurti forward, the question that becomes significant for educators is, how do we arrest the movement of the self to be truly free of the self?

A child or an adult who identifies only with the self, its desires, their fulfilment, perhaps without concern for others, is a self-centred person, seeking gratification, pleasure, fulfilment, often at great human cost. This kind of self-identification lacks an orientation to the world outside and lacks empathy or consideration for others or for the earth. This kind of self-identity is a concern only for a limited world without any concern or commitment for another world. At another level, identity is a sense of moving out of inner emptiness, the search to belong to something, or someone, whether another individual, a group, or community. The quest for the individual in search of identity is for one of sameness: the root meaning of the word identity is 'same'. An individual looks for the same, continuity, in those with whom identification is sought. There is a sense of sameness between the external world and an individual's own feelings, aspirations, and goals. This sense of sameness reflects an extension of the self within a group, a community, or an institution. It is somehow difficult to unravel identity as we are all caught up in it in one way or another.

An individual is looking for this connection, of affiliating to that which is similar, of how one views oneself, in relation to others. Such a sense of sameness gives an individual a sense of fulfilment, a satisfaction, a sense of all's well with the world, and also, a sense of purpose and commitment to life and what one attempts to make of it. The psychologist Sudhir Kakar tells us that

> Identity is meant to convey the process of synthesis between inner life and outer social reality as well as the feeling of personal continuity and consistency with oneself. It refers to the sense of having a stake in oneself, and at the same time, in some kind of confirming community.
>
> (Kakar 1981)

It is in the second part of Kakar's definition, that is, 'It refers to the sense of having a stake in oneself, and at the same time, in some kind of confirming community', that we can begin to understand how the individual gets trapped into different kinds of processes and practices that perhaps embolden particular linguistic, regional, religious, ideological, or national identities.

It is not always possible to change or break this strong sense of identity, because while it may be possible to begin to understand and attempt to transform psychological processes, it is a far greater challenge to do away with cultural and historical forces that are embedded in us as general dispositions. These general dispositions, our 'habitus' (Bourdieu 1977), are ways of thinking, acting, and being that are ingrained in us through processes of socialisation, become part of our consciousness and express our identity in particular and in general ways.

A child cultivates self-images through engagement with the environment and, through various experiences in childhood, develops a sense of identity. The most significant social institution in which the child is embedded is the family. It is the family that shapes, moulds, and in fact provides the emotional scaffolding within which children are not only enclosed but also provided the essential cultural and social baggage on which the child's understanding of the world rests. The family shapes the faith, beliefs, practices, ritual, or otherwise that influence the child and the eyes with which the child looks out at the social world.[2]

At the same time, despite the adverse circumstances of familial conditioning, some children are able to not be influenced or conditioned by the family even at a young age. The role of the school, and the people in it, is essential in also shaping the views of children and adolescents. In this sense, 'belonging' is not circumscribed by the religion, caste, community, family, or nation that one belongs to. If it is, we are identifying too closely with one aspect of our identity. We tend to see this aspect of our identity as overwhelmingly our whole identity. Contrarily, identity is not fixed; it is constant movement; there is a certain fluidity to identity. This finds expression most clearly in those who are on the move, lives of nomads, immigrants, and refugees who simultaneously inhabit different cultures, communities, nations, and move between identities in a naturally flexible manner, unknown often to themselves. The essence of identity, that is unbound, and open, without being rootless, constantly open to the changing movements that encapsulate our interdependent lives, of nature, identity in movement, fluid, swept into a storm, subsiding into a gentle wave, of a totality even in the vast expanse of the ocean.[3]

If we view ourselves as the ocean, our identities cannot be encased within a single or even multiple frames. They cannot be captured and encased as such. They remain flexible and fluid, merging with parts or the larger whole, retreating and silent, at other times, and in fact are a major force or source of defining us as humans in this vast space we inhabit on the earth. The centre within us is strong and untouched, but we scatter it in our identities that we strongly inhabit and defend through our need to belong, to be part of something that apparently gives us a sense of belonging, that feeds the emptiness within us, as in the poem by Pablo Neruda (n.d.).

The challenge is not so much to do away with identity but with identification, as has been suggested by Krishnamurti. He points out that although we recognise forms of external identifications, such as a flag, or a country or with religion, and cease to identify 'with' them, we still identify 'with' a strong sense of 'myself'. It is this robust sense of self that leads to my sense of 'identification with'. This is an illusion made up of images and words which we misrecognise as an objectively 'real' self. As Krishnamurti says,

> But the mind is afraid of being completely empty. Therefore, it says 'must be'. Now the mind never finds out what takes place if it really empty . . . because it is so afraid of being empty. Therefore, it must be occupied. . .
> (Krishnamurti 2019c: 13–14)

with this, that, and the other. Simultaneously, the mind becomes stronger through such forms of identification although it is not the 'freedom' that Krishnamurti proposes. He says,

> identification is essentially a thought process by which the mind safeguards and expands itself; and in becoming something it must resist and defend, it must own and discard. In this process of becoming, the mind or the self grows tougher and more capable; but this is not love.
> (Krishnamurti 2016: 74)

Identification in this sense puts an end to inquiry and to discovery. This makes it a 'vicarious experience, and hence utterly false' (Krishnamurti 2016: 75). In order to stay afloat, the mind is tethered to something, an identification with something or someone, an ideology, position, power, an institution, and such anchoring will not allow the freedom to experience or experiment with the unknown. In this sense, the mind cannot be free.

It is this strong identification with the self that leads to the nourishment and perpetuation of the self; that leads to the identification with ideas and what they represent; that leads also to an understanding that there is something other than these forms of connections that bring so much misery into our lives. And that we perhaps therefore need to transcend them. This leads to further conflict, and as Krishnamurti concludes, 'Thus we are in constant battle within ourselves'.

Krishnamurti points to the outcomes of strong identifications and indicates that these do not help in sustaining freedom and order in society. If anything, they result in division, engender conflict, and often end up with situations that celebrate war, terror, and violence.

In a discussion with students at Rishi Valley School, Krishnamurti's commitment to the ending of global violence and the important role of education in this process is clearly stated:

'JK: You have to be educated because you want to free the world from violence. Now: To free the world from violence, you must be free of violence yourself – mustn't you?
S: Yes, sir.
JK: Do you understand what I am saying?
S: Yes, sir.
JK: In order to free the world from violence, you must be free of violence. That is the meaning of education – and not you are violent and want the rest of the world to be free of violence. You are part of the world and, therefore, you have to be free from violence; only then you can help the world to be free of violence' (Krishnamurti, KFI Bulletin 2021: 24–25).

It is important to consider how this is to be brought about in an educational process for which Krishnamurti lays out no predetermined answers. Everything depends on the teachers and the quality of dialogue and engagement they bring to students and to life at school. Herzberger has commented,

> Krishnamurti believed that both nationalism and organized religion are basically divisive, because the sense of

identity they foster is exclusive. As Hindus, we define ourselves by rejecting others. In thus defining ourselves and rejecting others, we thrust our worst fears on to them. Thus a cycle of hatred and fear takes root which eventually leads to violence.

(Herzberger 1999)

All attachment to identities, particularly group identities, creates exclusion and difference and is therefore dangerous. Krishnamurti did not accept that allegiance to any of these was necessary to being a productive member of society. Instead, he urges us to understand that we constitute the 'rest of mankind' and are not disparate groups or individuals based on caste, creed, religion, language, race, ethnicity, or gender. Nationalism which expects loyalty and patriotism as twin aspects of commitment to a single national ideology cannot offer us that sense of being part of a larger humanity. All forms of group identities, and allegiance to one or other, need to be 'set aside in order to discover the deeper, more universal spirit that makes a whole out of a multitude of parts' (Herzberger 1999). Clinging to identities results in actions that are divisive, create conflict, and inevitably lead to war and violence. Krishnamurti is not arguing that we need to do away with identity altogether. Undoubtedly, we are part of the fabric of social life, and Krishnamurti is emphasising the dangers of being identified with one or the other aspect of life rather than with the whole of life. He repeatedly stresses the responsibility of human beings to others, to the earth, to life in all its forms of interconnectedness. We are not isolated individuals in society but a part of the web of humanity, disparate as it may be, but nonetheless united in our humanity.

It may appear that there is an idealism in a view that seeks to emphasise the natural goodness of all human beings over the mess that society has created for itself over centuries of movement for goals that represent avid self-interest and self-perpetuation. Krishnamurti called attention to the significant role of the individual in this process of change. He was well aware of the prevalent social factors that prevent the individual from being a prime agent in social transformation. One of the key factors is the fact of violence that has so engulfed the world. Violence, in various forms and meanings, is of increasing significance in our analysis of both everyday life and momentous personal and social change. Violence is included within categories and concepts variously related to power, state, politics, culture, and symbols. Alternatively, violence has also been analysed as a distinct phenomenon, as a non-reducible form of power. This has been referred to as 'structural violence'; a form of practice; a set of social institutions; with their own rhythms, dynamics, and practices.

The old ideas of the nature and directions of violence are being disturbed and challenged by more piercing forms of violence. At a recent event, the Buddhist scholar, Samdhong Rinpoche mentioned that in ancient times, the violence would end with the particular wars or conflicts over territory or foraging for resources. In modernity, however, violence has become a market, supported by an industry that perpetuates violence. While the field of violence encompasses war, terrorism, ethnic cleansing, domestic violence, violence against women, hate crimes, caste-based violence, communal riots, and the recent patterns of lynching and mob violence, there is an urgency to re-examine the subject, not merely as a 'theoretical exercise' but more in an attempt to understand and attempt transformation in the violent everyday world that we inhabit.

From being bizarre, violence has become an ongoing occurrence, naturalised, acquired a banal form and is seamlessly woven into the social fabric. Writing about the trial of Adolf Eichmann, one of the chief architects of the Holocaust, the philosopher Hannah Arendt refers to 'the banality of evil' and 'the normalization of human wickedness'. Her report on the trial is a sobering reflection on it as she says 'the lesson that this long course in human wickedness had taught us – the lesson of the fearsome, word-and-thought-defying banality of evil' (Arendt 2006). Lessons learnt during World War II and its aftermath have apparently not communicated this, because we have seen unprecedented violence in recent years. This kind of easy acceptance of a violent world further perpetuates the idea of the banality of violence. While there has been an increased visibility of violence, the simultaneous invisibilisation of its forms and manifestations helps us understand the ways in which violence has shifted from being an interpersonal mode of activity to an overarching theme of existence.[4]

At the same time, the memory of violence in different forms, which we may have witnessed, experienced, heard or read about, or visually seen through multiple mediums, is part of our consciousness and haunts us through an assemblage of images, the experience of pain, hurt, sorrow, distress, and trauma. Memory not only keeps violence alive in our consciousness but also plays a role in forming our identities in opposition to violence, or as perpetrators of violence, as keepers of justice, of how we imagine ourselves to be as those for example who will deliver justice to the poor, the unequal, and the marginalised. In that too, there is a sense of identity as the conscience-keeper and liberator of the dispossessed. Memory is a significant process of the mind, and we seek to come to the new, to break our identification with, from the same mind. This is a challenge: to contend with meeting the new (challenging identity and identification with) from the old (that is, the same mind, grounded in memory that regurgitates experience, identification with the self, and so on).

Krishnamurti's emphasis on the extreme violence prevalent in society is a way to help us understand the urgency with which we need to address issues of identification and violence. The educator Paulo Freire tells us:

> If the humanization of the oppressed signifies subversion, so also does their freedom; hence the necessity for constant control. And the more the oppressors control the oppressed the more they change them into apparently inanimate 'things'. This tendency of the oppressor consciousness to 'in-animate' everything and everyone it encounters, in its eagerness to possess, unquestionably corresponds with a tendency to sadism.
>
> (2005: 59)

The dangers of oppression by capitalism, of being consumers in a ruthlessly capitalist society where the market economy depends on excessive consumption, result in the de-humanisation of society and of humans being made into in-animate objects. That is why humanity succumbs so easily to greed over need, to being a consumer over a user, and in becoming a 'thing', propelled by the media, by popular culture and the massification of society, indulges in mindless activity, unaware and inattentive to either his or her own condition or that of humanity at large. Krishnamurti referred to the de-humanisation of society as an ugly aspect of social life that could not be resolved through recourse to 'non-violence'. He points out,

> we human beings are violent..., and this we never really go into because we have the concept of non-violence; we are concerned with the concept and ideology of non-violence, of what should be, but not with the fact of what actually is.
>
> (Krishnamurti 1967)

It is therefore essential that we first understand what makes us violent, both our inner processes and external factors, and that will lead to the ending of violence, not faith in an ideology of 'non-violence', however appealing it might be. For example, our most intimate relationships are often based on forms of violence, and it is possible that we do not even perceive such conflict as violence. Sometimes, we may seek help through counselling or continue to live with such conflict, viewing it as an inevitable part of everyday life. Krishnamurti however asserts, 'Every form of conflict is violence, not only the psychological conflict, within the skin, but also outwardly, in our relationships with other human beings, with society' (Krishnamurti 1967). To live with peace, as fully integrated human beings, we must therefore focus on the ending of violence. We need to do this through, as Krishnamurti says, observation of 'what is', not 'what should be'. There is an urgency with which an individual must act to deal with her psychological conflict that inevitably affects the external world. To understand this, one needs to connect to understanding oneself as well as the workings of the external world in relationship to us.

> There is war outwardly and war inwardly within each one of us, is it possible to end it immediately, psychologically turning your back on it? Nobody can answer that question except yourself . . . when you answer it, not depending on any authority, on any intellectual or emotional concepts or formulas or ideologies.
> (Krishnamurti 1967)

There is a tendency among those who seek to bring an end to violence and work for change to have faith in an alternative system, an ideology, or a leader who would perhaps be able to organise and set in motion a collective movement against injustice, or inequalities of different kinds or work for the ending of violence, particularly among the marginalised and excluded. While such endeavours serve a purpose, to better working conditions, focus on human rights issues and set in motion trends towards establishing new laws focusing on the rights of the poor, lower caste, marginalised, and oppressed, Krishnamurti was not sure if these were able to transform society and establish a different world order. To bring about lasting peace, it is essential, for Krishnamurti, to first contend with the violence within us and in our relationships and thereby seek to change our relationship with the world. Krishnamurti therefore considers faith in someone else, a Guru, a leader, a revolutionary, an ideology as a crutch, to overcome that which we lack, our own inability to question or examine our actions and their outcomes. We may have faith in a religion, in a nation, and in a leader, and it will bring us to the challenging and uneasy situation that many societies including India find themselves in. Faith is a 'weapon of the weak', to use James Scott's evocative term (Scott 1985); it is what keeps one tethered to that which will definitely bring conflict, divisiveness, and sorrow. Faith in an ideology of whatever kind is a narrow and sectarian approach to understanding the vast canvas of life. To be free from faith, one needs to abandon the attachments we cling to, whether of the social institutions in which we are embedded or from the political or religious moorings we connect to. Krishnamurti wanted to be free from all such attachments: from organisations, institutions, and even from the people he was close to. He emphasised the importance of being completely open to life around us, 'To have no resistance, to have no barriers inwardly towards anything, to be really free, completely, from all the minor urges, compulsions, and demands, with all their little conflicts and hypocrisies, is to walk in life with open arms' (Krishnamurti 2000a: 69).

Having disavowed all movements and revolutions, Krishnamurti saw the possibilities of a transformed future lying in the right kind of education. Such an education would not be based on tradition and the past. Undoubtedly, knowledge and skills require some reference to conventional knowledge and that is necessary for education. Krishnamurti was concerned about the whole individual, not a fragmented human being, focused only on garnering academic knowledge. Academic knowledge was based on memory and education ensured the reproduction of that knowledge through evaluation methods that tested only memory recall. Krishnamurti argued:

> And mind is memory, at whatever level, by whatever name you call it; mind is the product of the past, it is founded on the past, which is memory, a conditioned state. Now, with that memory we meet life, we meet a new challenge. The challenge is always new, and our response is always old because it is the outcome of the past. So, experiencing without memory is one state, and experiencing with memory is another. That is, there is a challenge, which is always new. I meet it with the response, with the condition of the old. So, what happens? I absorb the new, I do not understand it, and the experiencing of the new is conditioned by the past. Therefore, there is a partial understanding of the new, there is never complete understanding. It is only when there is complete understanding of anything that it does not leave the scar of memory. . . . The situation in the world at the present time demands a new approach, a

> new way of tackling the world problem, which is ever new. We are incapable of approaching it anew because we approach it with our conditioned minds, with national, local, family, and religious prejudices. That is, our previous experiences are acting as a barrier to the understanding of the new challenge, so we go on cultivating and strengthening memory, and therefore we never understand the new, we never meet the challenge fully, completely. It is only when one is able to meet the challenge anew, afresh, without the past, only then does it yield its fruits, its riches.
>
> (Krishnamurti 1948)

Education must help us to understand the freshness of observation as it is, without the layer of memory, to observe nature, an experiment in the laboratory, as well as our own fears and anxieties with the same quality of looking that enables us to see 'what is'. In other words, to see ourselves as we are without the layers of obfuscation that cloud our understanding of the self, in relationship with others, including the earth.

Education, Responsibility, and Transformation

> Education is meant to cultivate the responsibility of a human being who is confronted with the horrors of wars. Are you going to fit into all that violence, brutality? Do you understand what I am asking you? Education is meant to bring about in you the sense of unity, the sense of life as a whole.
>
> (Krishnamurti 2021: 6)

To repeat an oft-quoted sentence from Krishnamurti, 'we are the world and the world is us'. Even if acts of physical violence are taking place elsewhere, we are witness to such violence, through the media, through our engagement as social beings, and cannot deny responsibility towards the ending of this violence in one way or another. Krishnamurti often reiterated his axiomatic statement: You are the World. It is not enough to understand this theoretically but to experience it viscerally, with every fibre of one's being, 'to feel that, to be totally committed to it, and to nothing else, brings about a feeling of great responsibility and an action that must not be fragmentary but whole' (Krishnamurti 2017a: 66). What does this mean: 'a feeling of great responsibility and an action that must not be fragmentary but whole'? Does a focus on the self, and doing away with self-identification, imply a fragmentary approach? Krishnamurti did not seek to address external 'reform' because 'reform, however necessary, only breeds the need for further reform and there is no end to it. What is needed is revolution in man's thinking, not patchwork reform' (Krishnamurti 1961: 45). He poses the question,

> If one may ask, what do you mean when you talk about acting politically? Is political action, whatever that may be, separate from the total action of man, or is it part of it? . . . A tree is the root, the trunk, the branch, the leaf, the flower. Any action which is not comprehensive, total, must inevitably lead to sorrow. There is only total human action, not political action, religious action, or Indian action. Action which is separative, fragmentary, always leads to conflict both within and without.
> (Krishnamurti 1961: 45)

On being probed further by the questioner who seems to think that Krishnamurti is suggesting that political action is impossible, Krishnamurti responds,

> Not at all. The comprehension of total action surely does not prevent political, educational or religious activity. These are not separate activities, they are all part of a unitary process which will express itself in different directions. What is important is this unitary process, and not a separate political action, however apparently beneficial.
> (Krishnamurti 1961: 45)

It is through such an integrated approach, holism in education, and of which 'self-knowledge' is a critical component that Krishnamurti sought to bring about transformation. This would in turn lead to a change in our relationship to people, nature, objects, and ideas. Krishnamurti argued that our minds are so conditioned that we are unable to look, listen, or learn without our prior knowledge that foregrounds the role of memory and time. He therefore highlighted the need to work with young children whose minds are fresh, and free of the burden of memory, excessive knowledge, or already ingrained ways of acting, thinking, and being.

Before climate change activism became an urgent necessity for sustainable life on the planet, Krishnamurti's most impassioned pleas for saving the planet addressed climate change that is an irreversible global reality. His vision for a transformed world included an understanding of how we relate to nature, the environment, and its resources. In a talk to children at Rishi Valley, Krishnamurti asked them,

> Is education to cultivate the great responsibility that each one of us has in living in this world – the responsibility towards nature, to trees, the mountains, the earth, the beauty of the land, the animals upon the earth, the minerals? Is it, also, to feel responsible for human beings' wasteful using up of the earth? Part of our education is to feel a responsibility for all this – that is, to feel totally responsible as a human being living in this world, not only to nature, to the world outside in which we live but, also, to feel a responsibility in our relationship to each other.
>
> (Krishnamurti 2021: 5)

There is an inherent violence in the manner in which the earth has been ravaged by humanity based on insatiable greed, materialism, and avarice. Krishnamurti believed that it is the task of education to help children become aware of this and develop a sense of responsibility towards the earth and nature. This will play a significant role in bringing about a change in attitudes towards the earth and one another, thereby enabling a harmonious relationship between all aspects of nature including humanity.

At several times, at his talks with children and adults, Krishnamurti emphasised this relationship with nature, and the need to care for and nurture the earth. He argued that we have a utilitarian relationship to the earth, 'utilizing it for our convenience. . . . If one really loved the earth, there would be frugality in using the things of the earth' (Krishnamurti 2016: 45). We don't even try to understand our relationship with nature which is as complex as our relationship to our closest kin, he would say, 'We never actually stop and love the earth or the things of the earth' (Krishnamurti 2016: 45). Krishnamurti believed that if we did not have a relationship with the earth, we could not have a relationship with nature or with animals and would thereby would 'lose the touch of life'. He cautioned his audience that caring for the earth with one's own hands is essential but is done by 'only the lower castes' (in India) and 'we are ashamed to work with our hands' and have therefore lost our relationship to nature (Krishnamurti 2016: 45). Krishnamurti was well aware that misusing the earth's resources and a lack of relationship with nature would result in irreversible damage to the ecosystem and to the planet. At the same time, Krishnamurti was not suggesting a return to some ideal way of life, which perhaps did not exist. As Robert Kaplan has put it, Krishnamurti 'eschewed utopianism, he scoffed at a return to pastoral beatitude' as these were blind to the cruelty, competition, and divisiveness in the world (1996: 356). Kaplan goes further and suggests, following the environmental security expert, Daniel Deudney, that Krishnamurti perhaps 'foresaw a historical phase in which people would identify with. . . "green culture" or "earth nationalism" . . . which may perhaps result in the "global management" of a vast array of environmental challenges in the future' (Kaplan 1996: 356). In fact, Kaplan goes so far as to suggest that 'Krishnamurti's ideas may be thought of as a precursor to the "Gaia" theory . . . which sees the Earth as a living system in which living and non-living forms continuously interact' (Kaplan 1996: 356).

The Krishnamurti schools are located in natural surroundings, and children are encouraged to engage with nature and the environment through both curricular and extra-curricular activities that include working with the hands, caring for the earth, trees, plants, nurturing biodiversity, sustainability and thus form unique bonds with nature that in many ways perhaps last a lifetime.

Krishnamurti has often been critiqued by social activists and others about his lack of attention to the less privileged, marginalised people of India.[5] At one time, Krishnamurti posed the question, 'Is there justice at all?' and adds,

> We want justice. We see victims of injustice, victims who are neurotic, victims who are psychopathic and those of us who are born to poverty and struggle, struggle for the rest of our lives. . . . Should we not talk, not of justice, not trying to bring about equality, but of compassion?
>
> (Krishnamurti 1982: 15)

This does not mean that Krishnamurti was against justice or equality but saw the pervasiveness of inequality and deep injustice that prevails in human relations across society. While some forms of structural oppression exist from which we must seek freedom, in a deeper sense, there is injustice in every form of human relationship. Basing action on an ideological resolution to the problem was not of much lasting use. For Krishnamurti, compassion, and the action that leads from it, is essential to personal relations and to social life. His own compassion for the poor, the working class, the marginalised, and excluded is well known to those who worked closely with him, and spent time in his company. This was characteristic of his view that in order to work with the marginalised and seek to end injustice, we must be able to perceive it with compassion that results in immediate action.

In a dialogue with students at the Rishi Valley School, a student asks him, 'The world is full of callous people, indifferent people, cruel people, and how can you change those people?'.

Krishnamurti's response draws attention to one's responsibility to first 'put one's house in order', as he often said, before attempting to change others:

> The world is full of callous people, indifferent people, cruel people, and how can you change those people? Is that it? Why do you bother about changing others? Change yourself, isn't it? Because, if you grow up, you will also become callous, you will also become indifferent, you will also become cruel, because the past generation is vanishing, they are going, and you are coming, and if you also prove callous, indifferent, cruel, you will also be the same society. So, first don't bother about others. . . . What matters is that you change, that you are not callous, that you are not indifferent.
>
> (Krishnamurti 2000b: 14)

The responsibility for change rests primarily with every individual and Krishnamurti sought to communicate this to his audience, children, or adults.

Krishnamurti did not seek allegiance to any political movement, organisation, or ideological perspective. As he did not subscribe to any ideological position whatsoever, he did not need to wave a flag or continuously refer to caste, gender, or class inequalities. He did not consider it necessary to repeatedly emphasise that equity is essential to social life. In his talks and writings, Krishnamurti was concerned about all of humankind that encompassed the marginalised, the poor, the excluded, as well as the Brahmin, the upper classes, the privileged.

It is because he talked to his large audiences around the world only in English; it would appear that he therefore addressed only those similar to him in caste, class, and privilege. There was not only one kind of 'class' present in his audience. It was a heterogeneous group of people who would show up to listen to him, and it is also true that his audiences varied in the different cities he spoke in. The audience in his public meetings was always mixed, children, men, and women, some with their caste marks on their foreheads, others in Western clothes, several young people, students, writers, poets, seekers, including young Westerners, and many workers, who perhaps did not understand the English but wanted to be in his presence, touch him as he left the dais, and seek his blessings. It is somewhat inadequate and perhaps meaningless to judge them all to be like Krishnamurti, akin to his privileged background.[6]

To bring about a social transformation, we need to first contend with the several social and cultural factors that mitigate and impede change. These include the ways in which gender inequalities and violence against women dominate the social landscape in both urban and rural India, the marginal and excluded position of Dalits and adivasis across the country, the increasingly state-sponsored or legitimised acts of violation of human rights in conflict areas, the blatant corruption, lack of governance, and apathy that inhibit social transformation. As social beings, we cannot remain immune, and while we may not seek a social revolution, we need to be present in the social moment as much as in our quest for transformation.

Krishnamurti did not reject this kind of action and in fact often urged his audience to not be mere passive observers but do something. His first and most pressing concern was for the neighbours of his schools in India, who were mostly the rural poor,

> First of all, I would get all the villagers together, and explain to them that we're going to have schools for their children. We'll see that we get enough money; we'll work for it. We'll say: 'We'll build; you help us to build'. That's one thing I would do: schools for them. And I would also see to the agriculture and all that side of it very clearly, definitely – expert work.
> (Krishnamurti, KFI Bulletin 1995: 20)

Krishnamurti questioned the children in his schools, in his meetings with them, by asking them if they cared for those workers who cared for them, for the villagers whose paths they may cross during the day, for others less privileged than themselves.

How would they care for them if they did not even understand their lives, he would ask.

> Go around and look at all the terrible villages you have around you. Look at the poverty. Must not you look at all this, must not you understand all this? You can't understand this through mere books, by merely getting a great many degrees; you have to feel; you have to see, you have to observe. That means, we have to be educated totally, all round.
> (Krishnamurti 2021: 6)

Krishnamurti was confident that if children were provided an integrated education, the possibilities for change were endless. Confirming the individual's role in bringing about social equity, he said, 'the fullest development of every individual brings about a society of equals. The present social struggle to bring about equality on the economic or some spiritual level has no meaning at all' (Krishnamurti 1987a: 4). At the same time, Krishnamurti acknowledged that there is the possibility of change through mass movements or collective struggle, but this could not last unless there is a 'psychological revolution' in individuals. At a talk in Madanapalle in 1939, he said, 'Perhaps a new organisation, through mass-action, through legislation, may remove economic domination. But psychologically your whole intellectual values are based on power; and as long as the pursuit of power exists, you must create conflict in relationship' (Krishnamurti, KFI Bulletin 2020: 9). It is essential that these are closely examined, and Krishnamurti believed that the right kind of education that is based on self-inquiry, and helps students and educators address their emotions and feelings (in addition to sharpening their intellect), will bring about a different kind of human being. It is such human beings who will bring about a social transformation, not violent revolution based on divisive ideologies that seek to emphasise one form of 'change' over another.

Krishnamurti relentlessly pushed students and educators to look outside their own petty little concerns at the beauty of nature, to care for the earth, plant trees, be connected to nature.

He pushed teachers to be related to children, not to judge them, but to understand them through the right kind of relationship that was based more on a kind of intimate communication than on the hierarchy between a teacher and student. Both teachers and students in Krishnamurti's view are learners together, seeking to understand themselves and the world through relationship. Education is not only about academic growth and an intellectual life but also more importantly about self-inquiry in which both the teacher and the student are equal participants.

Social transformation is not a simple process. Agency cannot remain a personal, individual 'phenomenon' and is in fact connected to the pursuit of ethics for 'goodness' in the global human condition. This opens up possibilities through an expanded understanding of how we perceive and engage with the world. In our understanding of the contemporary human condition, we can no longer be passive observers in a deeply divided and self-destructive world. We must not perpetuate passivity, docility, or silence. We need to be engaged social actors, in whatever way we see fit, if we wish to see change move. Along with our processes of watching the self, and forms of self-identification, it is important to also express concern through engagement with civil society that we must strengthen with our support, and with whom, we can question and perhaps redress the banality of violence, the mindless consumption, the inordinate corruption, all of which spiral into what we consider a decaying and dying world.

It is precisely because we view ourselves as having independent individual existence that we fail to see the interconnectedness of humanity, and of humanity with nature and the planet earth. We need to give up our sense of identification and feel the oneness of the human mind, or, as Samdhong Rinpoche puts it, 'the wholeness of universal consciousness' (Rinpoche 2019). This implies, as Krishnamurti emphasised, the development of a global outlook that shuns linguistic or religious affiliations, regionalism, nationalism, and the like. The importance of the individual as a separate, consuming identity has been created by the forces of modernity, capitalism, and globalisation. The individual who has the ability and resources to mindlessly consume, and not pause to understand the consequences of this consumption, is the same individual who must first unravel the processes that not only enable one to be a consumer but also understand the effects of this on a global scale.

In this context, what can be the role of education in this process of transformation and in restoring humanism to humanity? Krishnamurti's profound legacy in education has been the establishment of schools in India and abroad for the transformation of the human mind and consciousness, in order to bring about a change in individuals and in society. Education is not an objective instrument but a deeply nuanced method for the transformation of consciousness and social change. Education is viewed as the medium through which we can attain not just knowledge, academic skills, and abilities but also gain the quality of critical discernment so that we do not succumb to the violence that has become endemic to our existence. The question that educators encounter pertains to the methods by which the quality of critical discernment may be achieved in a space that itself harbours violence and extreme forms of self-identification.

The relationship between education and violence is well established. We can see how school curricula have been used to justify violence. For example, the discipline of history which is part of the school curriculum emphasises a particular society, a nation, and carves out the idea of a nation, an identity that involves a curation of events, of memories that legitimise what it means to be an Indian or a Pakistani. Studies of history textbooks in the subcontinent have shown how the process of exclusion and 'othering' are drawn out and in doing so, not only justify but also may glorify acts of violence, systematic discrimination, marginalisation, and exclusion.[7]

Similarly, citizenship is built through education once again emphasising loyalty and patriotism in the context of a single nation. Nationalism is not merely an idea but becomes a virtue, a project, and to defend the contours, whether territorial, imagined, or rhetorical, of what constitutes a nation becomes an essential component of educational practice. This is done through not only the curriculum but also more powerfully through symbolism that deeply penetrates a child's consciousness, through song, music, drawing, writing, and sports, every kind of activity within educational practice wherein we establish the nation as an entity in the hearts and minds of children.[8] Symbols of the nation-state develop the theme of nationalism in our consciousness and become part of the collective unconscious over a period of time through repetition and continuous daily practice. It is this everyday violence that has a deep impact on young minds who eventually succumb to the pressures of modern nation-state. We may thus conclude that education has been part of the process of the imagination, construction, and transaction of violence through curricular and pedagogic practices that emphasise separation, exclusion, and difference. This enhances the sense of identification among children and young adults with particular subjects, particular sports, particular careers, and so on. Children are not permitted to be seekers but to fit into slots which may have been made more flexible or enabling but are nevertheless, slots.

The question we need to ask is whether it is possible to overcome the impact of this education in our own lives and in those of our children and the society we inhabit. Are there ways to understand the processes of healing and transformation through education? How can a dialogue around education, engagement, and transformation through young children reconfigure the way through which lot of what is happening in contemporary society may be understood? As educators, it is essential to therefore examine our intent and processes of working with children in schools. We need to begin, as Krishnamurti says, with ourselves, examine our own inner processes, and understand the processes that lead to identification and violence in our everyday lives.

There is an apparent idealism in a view that seeks to emphasise the natural goodness of all human beings over the mess that society has created for itself over centuries of movement for goals that represent avid self-interest and self-perpetuation. Krishnamurti called attention to the significant role of the individual in this process of change. Radhika Herzberger (2015) locates her understanding of Krishnamurti's perspective in the context of the Rishi Valley School, in rural Andhra Pradesh. She examines Krishnamurti's perspective as enabling individuals to discover the ethics of a new way of life which is essential for the renewal of society. For him, education lay at the centre of the change that was possible. Krishnamurti made a clear distinction between a system of education based on building knowledge as opposed to one that, as Herzberger puts it, 'is nourished by an awakening of the senses, and the observation of both the inner and the outer worlds'. The education Krishnamurti proposed was for the whole of humanity; it was to develop 'total responsibility': to the earth, nature and to one another undivided by nationalism, and religion, for example. Talking to students, he said,

> What is happening in the world is a projection of what is happening inside each one of us; what we are, the world is. Most of us are in turmoil, we are acquisitive, possessive, we are jealous and condemn people; and that is exactly what is happening in the world, only more dramatically, ruthlessly.
> (Krishnamurti, KFI Bulletin 2018b: 2)

He asks them to be concerned about this as much as they are about learning new concepts or with the passing of examinations. It is our total responsibility to care about the world and do something about it. This idea of complete responsibility is linked to Krishnamurti's oft-cited statement, 'You are the world': for Krishnamurti, to live is to be related and in this sense, education is about developing and nurturing relationships through learning that are not based on the acquisition of knowledge alone. It is an education that is based on virtue and personal ethics, and moving from the personal into the public space, leading to change and transformation in society.

The 'Religious' Mind in Education

Mark Lee, who set up the Krishnamurti Oak Grove School in Ojai, California, at Krishnamurti's behest, shares with us that Krishnamurti's underlying concern was to establish a school that was concerned with 'religious education'. He said to Mark Lee, 'Perhaps in one generation we can make a difference and produce young people who will change themselves and the world – sensitive, aware and caring [people] who will lead religious lives' (Krishnamurti, as quoted in Lee 2015: 136). Krishnamurti did not use the term 'religion' in the sense of organised religion with its institutional character, dogmas, beliefs, or rituals. Religion and religiosity could not be about authority, tradition, or the conditioning that enforced normative behaviour, adhering to certain 'moral' values and practices that apparently reflect a 'religious way of life'. Krishnamurti tells us that,

> the true religious mind . . . does not belong to any cult, to any group, to any religion, to any organised church. . . . The religious mind is completely alone. . . . Not being nationalistic, not being conditioned by its environment, such a mind has no horizons, no limits. It is explosive, new, young, fresh, innocent.
> (Krishnamurti 2018a: 17)

Krishnamurti envisaged the 'religious mind' as being central to the educational endeavour that the Krishnamurti schools are engaged in. If this was not the goal of his schools, he wanted to have nothing to do with them. He said one day in May 1985, about nine months before his passing, in conversation with Mark Lee,

> what is going to happen to this school, [the Oak Grove School in Ojai], the other schools in the future? Will they become sectarian, potty little institutions where only rich parents send their children? Can you keep the religious mind alive here? They will be successful, top schools, but who cares about that? That kind of success is cheap . . . Have you listened to me, do you know what it means to have a religious mind? You have to do this here . . . otherwise it is not worth it. It is a waste of time. Unless you are doing it, get out of it, leave.
> (Lee 2015: 258)

Elsewhere, in a brief note on 'If I were Head of Rishi Valley School', Krishnamurti advocates, 'I would talk a great deal about religion – the spirit of religion, not the circus of religion. I would talk about affection; forget religion. I would talk about the quality of affection' (Krishnamurti 1995: 21). Krishnamurti is well aware that children are cynical about religion and dismissive of it as a resource for themselves or the world in general. He suggests therefore that teachers/educators need to approach it in the right way, helping them understand the religious spirit through a quality of affection that is not based on individual likes or dislikes.[9]

It is not easy to completely understand Krishnamurti's emphasis on the 'religious' mind. Herzberger has emphasised,

> For Krishnamurti [it] is one that is not based on belief or dogma, a well-established identity or books, but it is this quality of exploration. . . . Affection, a sense of beauty, a sense of truthfulness, all those are religious qualities, but they should be related to sensibility rather than to rules, regulations. . . . So, this sensibility comes through relationship. . . . But this has to be reinforced through the curriculum.
>
> (Herzberger, as cited in Kuyper 2014: 46)

This implies the significance of relationship and the curriculum in the lives of participants in Krishnamurti schools. An equal emphasis is laid on both aspects, relationship and curriculum, and for Herzberger, it is important to focus on how the religious mind can be interpreted in an educational context (Herzberger, as cited in Kuyper 2014: 47). Engaging with the children on themes that emerge from the religious mind is an essential aspect of the curriculum that is systematically and creatively worked out in educational practice.

In a talk to a group of students at Rishi Valley School, Krishnamurti (2018a) seeks to bring the urgent necessity of change to the attention of students as well as points to the quality of mind that is significantly different from the mind created by knowledge alone. This is the 'creative' mind, a mind that is not cluttered with the baggage of excessive knowledge including the memory of being hurt, and nor, as he puts it, is it 'greedy' or 'envious'.

It is a fresh mind, a mind that is vibrant and free, and is therefore able to deal with life differently. In that sense, it is a truly religious mind. For Krishnamurti, the religious mind is one that is free from any religious ideology or practice and concerned only with daily life in its entirety. This is the ethical mind that will result in what Krishnamurti refers to as 'right action' which will produce a society that is based on the essential goodness of human beings in society. Action cannot, however, be planned and executed in a fragmented or piecemeal manner: 'The seeing is the doing, and knowledge, because of its time quality, prevents the instant action. The religious mind has this quality of immediate action' (Krishnamurti, KFI Bulletin 1973a: 14). It is then imperative, as Krishnamurti sees it, that

> a different kind of education is necessary – not the mere cultivation of memory with all its emphasis on compulsion, conformity, imitation leading to violence, but the total culture of man in which the you and the me disappear and are not replaced by the state or by a new figure of sanctity. This different education is concerned with knowledge, with freedom, with what is and to go beyond what is.
> (Krishnamurti, KFI Bulletin 1973a: 14)

Krishnamurti is therefore not doing away with knowledge per se but emphasising that a focus on knowledge alone is a limited educational exercise.

The religious spirit and the scientific spirit must go together in the educational process envisioned by Krishnamurti. The scientific mind is also without dogma, 'moves from fact to fact', and 'has nothing to do with individual conditions, with nationalism, with race, with prejudice' (Krishnamurti 2018a: 16–17). It is a combination of the scientific mind and the religious mind that will together create 'a good world'. For Krishnamurti, the 'purpose of education is to create this new mind, which . . . does not conform to a pattern society has set' (Krishnamurti 2018a: 17). Such an education endeavours to help children and young adults understand their psychological processes through a scientific mind that can examine them through observation, without condemnation or self-flagellation. This kind of education would ensure the upbringing of a human being who knows compassion and in Krishnamurti's words 'knows what it is to be alive' (Krishnamurti 2018a: 18). Krishnamurti's approach to education therefore clearly emphasises the development of both the scientific and religious spirits for a complete human being, or an integrated human being, if you will. This is perhaps how we may understand Krishnamurti's perspective on holistic education.

Holistic Education

Holistic education has been often cited as the best approach to education of children's all-round development. It was suggested in the 1970s and 1980s, primarily in the United States, as an alternative to the heavily focused attention being paid to academic learning in schools. An instrumental approach to education and learning was sought to be therefore replaced by a more holistic and integrated approach that included elements from cognitive, emotional, and all-round physical development of children.[10] While Krishnamurti did not subscribe to any particular stream of thought, his perspective on education and learning has been viewed as holistic. Krishnamurti argued, 'The highest function of education is to bring about an integrated individual who is capable of dealing with life as a whole. The idealist, like the specialist, is not concerned with the whole, but only with a part' (Krishnamurti 2019a: 21). There is a limited understanding that grows out of pursuit of the 'ideal pattern', especially in education, however worthwhile it may be. A child therefore cannot be educated according to an idealistic perspective, as that would be conforming to an already set pattern rooted in an ideal, which would limit a child's potential. By wanting a child conform to an image, educators are not only putting restrictions on a child's abilities but also creating conflict as a child then has to fulfil expectations which may clash with what she is. In other words, ideals are a hindrance to our working with children in educational settings.

Krishnamurti did not quite perceive holistic education in the same way as other scholars. In a discussion with educators, he asks,

> Do you understand the word 'holistic'? To be 'holistic' is to be whole, to be good. The word 'good' means 'well put together': The mind that has been well put together, carefully, with diligence, which has the capacity to perceive the whole of man, and act from that. Now, can we as educators, living in this country or abroad, bring this about?
>
> (Krishnamurti 2011: 5)

It is therefore important to create a 'religious' spirit which is engaged in understanding oneself through relationship.

> Religious education in the true sense is to encourage the child to understand his own relationship to people, to things and to nature. There is no existence without relationship; and without self-knowledge, all relationship, with the one and with the many, brings conflict and sorrow.
>
> (Krishnamurti 2019a: 34)

Education, as Krishnamurti said, is not only about memorising some facts or about reading some book. It is about the whole of life and such an education enables a child to be engaged in living, in her relationships with people, nature, ideas, and things. The teacher and parent need to help the child understand that the accumulation of academic knowledge alone does not constitute education.

In 1967, a teacher at the Rishi Valley School asked Krishnamurti:

> much of our so-called education is concerned with the cultivation of the intellect, of reasoning, of the thinking faculty and also with the accumulation of knowledge. We seem to give very little attention to what one would

> call feeling. People do it a little through art, music and so on; but even there, they are more concerned with form rather than the experience of beauty. Could we discuss the question of having a feeling, whether it is for something, a truth or for a plant?
>
> (Krishnamurti, KFI Bulletin 1972: 2)

Krishnamurti agrees,

> the over-cultivation of the brain, in the sense intellect, destroys sensitivity. It is like developing, a very, very strong right arm; the left arm becomes weak. Is it possible to have a good brain and at the same time to have this passion? Passion comes into being with total self-abandonment.
>
> (Krishnamurti, KFI Bulletin 1972: 3)

For Krishnamurti, the focus in education needs to be not merely on academic knowledge but on knowing oneself. In his talks, Krishnamurti often used the metaphor of a carriage drawn by two horses where each horse is going in a different direction. One represents academic knowledge, the other psychological development. By paying attention to, and over-emphasising, the academic aspect alone (as we are still doing in schools across India), education is incomplete.

Krishnamurti was saying all this long before neuroscientists started telling us that the emotional development of children was part of their cognitive development and crucial to their learning or when Social Emotional Learning (SEL) became fashionable and de rigeur in educational practice. SEL as we know it is a method that works from the outside inwards. As stated on their website, 'Social and emotional competencies *can be taught, modelled, and practiced* and lead to positive student outcomes that are important for success in school and in life'.[11] The emphasis on teaching emotional competencies without a serious effort at self-understanding by teachers and students may perhaps result in a competency being developed. It is not based first and foremost on a process of self-inquiry in which the teacher and the student are equally involved. Later, in 2020, SEL website modified its definition as follows:

> Social and emotional learning (SEL) is an integral part of education and human development. SEL is the process through which all young people and adults acquire and apply the knowledge, skills and attitudes to develop healthy identities, manage emotions and achieve personal and collective goals, feel and show empathy for others, establish and maintain supportive relationships, and make responsible and caring decisions.[12]

This definition once again posits the *acquisition and application* of knowledge, skills, and attitudes. For Krishnamurti, the important starting point is that of self-inquiry into one's consciousness, into that which shapes our conduct. It is significant that Krishnamurti described the 'stream of consciousness' as thought-feeling. This guiding principle creates possibilities for enriching and nurturing emotional learning in school education. Paying attention to emotions, recognising them, being aware of them, and dealing with them becomes an important component of pedagogy. Through this, children learn to not only manage their emotions but also build certain social abilities and skills. Paying attention to what he called 'thought-feeling' was an important part of educational practice for Krishnamurti. At a talk in Ojai, 1945, Krishnamurti suggested to his audience,

> as a means to self-knowledge and right thinking, . . . one should write down every thought-feeling, the pleasant as well as the unpleasant. Thus one becomes aware of the whole content of consciousness, the private thoughts and secret motives, intentions and bondages. Thus through constant self-awareness there comes self-knowledge which brings about right thinking. For without self-knowledge there can be no understanding. The source of understanding is within oneself and there is no

comprehension of the world and your relationship to it without deep self-knowledge.

(Krishnamurti 1945)

He warned not to 'treat this writing down as a new method, a new technique', and to keep in mind that the essential thing is 'to become aware of every thought-feeling'. He concluded by saying, 'it is this discovery, this understanding that is the liberating and transforming factor' (Krishnamurti, as cited in Zwart 2012). To feel out each thought and feeling, it is the teacher's task to help children to do this. Being aware of one's thought-feeling, aware of the many layers of the educated consciousness brings about the transformation. One way to do this is to ask students (and teachers) to write down what they feel and think, and go over what they write later, to begin to understand their stream of consciousness. This is not merely a form of diary writing but an essential part of learning for children and for teachers to understand how their own consciousness works. This learning about oneself, one's thoughts and emotions, the stream of consciousness, as Krishnamurti put it, is transformative in both potential and practice. This also aids in developing relationships with one another in school.

Willem Zwart writes about his experience with children at Oak Grove School, Ojai:

> I asked the students to destroy the pages with their recorded thoughts and feelings and to write a short, reflective essay on the experience. At first, the exercise was not easy for students. One student wrote, 'It's strange to take the time to sit down and analyse your thoughts. It takes you deeper than just the first assumption you had about a certain thought. . . . It allows for the realization that a lot of your thoughts are superficial'. Another student found it not at all a pleasant experience: 'Well, to my surprise, as I sat on a rock below an oak tree there was so much . . . it soon became overwhelming. Thought after thought, page after page, it all made absolutely no sense. I guess I had never actually

tried to observe my thoughts in such a way'. A third student was dismayed to discover, 'how self-centred I am, when left alone with my own thoughts. I wonder if this is how others feel too. I noticed that many things that I wrote down had to do with *me*'.

Gradually, however, frustration gave way to learning. Students expressed amazement at the speed and seemingly random nature of their thoughts; observed that there appeared to be a link between their thoughts and the environment they were in; and noticed that by really attending to their thoughts and feelings they would sometimes end. As one student put it: 'It provided me with the opportunity to take a step back and assess a certain situation and all of my feelings as well. It allowed me to express all my disappointment, anger, frustration, and sadness. And then, after processing all of that, I could let it go. It was over and done. The issue suddenly became insignificant'. Several students echoed the sentiment that upon closer observation, the attachment to, and identification with thought became less pronounced or disappeared altogether.

(Zwart 2012)

Learning about one's own thought-feelings by writing them down helps us not only to connect to ourselves but also to understand our emotions, and how they are connected to our behaviour, environment, actions, and the overall culture at school.

Krishnamurti started schools with a purpose: to bring about a new generation of human beings who would be free of the conditioning of knowledge, and the past, and be able to look at life anew, in relationship to others, including nature and ideas, in an environment that was not grounded in fear or authority. He eschewed competition or comparison and asked teachers to create an ethos that was based on trust, affection, and openness. Discipline for Krishnamurti did not mean wielding the cane, or to exercise authority, to make children fear us and conform out of a sense of obedience. Instead, he expected relationship between teachers and students, among teachers, among children, to be the *sine qua non* of the culture of the school. Out of that relationship would emerge a sense of responsibility through which children could understand their own actions and behaviour. Self-inquiry is a method Krishnamurti espoused as part of an education that is not only about academic subjects but also about life itself.

Krishnamurti schools are trying to help students understand themselves, and may or may not be successful but the process is important. It is in the unfolding of the process, in the relationships that inhere at school, that Krishnamurti's vision may be transmitted. While Krishnamurti's focus in his talks and writings is no doubt on the child and young student, the teacher is critical to the process of educational transformation. In his talks to teachers, Krishnamurti exhorts them to have 'the long vision' despite having to respond immediately to the present, to what is happening in the immediate present (Krishnamurti 2018a: 84). This means keeping the mind young, never allowing oneself to be burdened by the weight of experience, tradition, which is a form of 'decay' and causes stagnation. Krishnamurti argues, 'It is a very delicate thing, a subtle thing, to have capacity and not to be a slave to it, to respond immediately to things you have to respond to, and to have this extraordinary depth and height and width' (Krishnamurti 2018a: 87). Keeping the mind fresh, young, and flexible ensures the teacher's 'long vision' and lies at the heart of what Krishnamurti considers 'right' education.

Such 'long vision' is surely to not only enhance and shape the teacher's attitude and modes of interaction with students, and others in school, but also develop her relationship with the subject she teaches, her pedagogic approach, and all other aspects of her functioning in school. In working with a 'long vision', the teacher's influence will be felt most on the children she mentors and nurtures, and her attitude will no doubt shape the worldviews and perspectives of young students at school.

Teachers in Krishnamurti schools do not merely 'teach'; instead, they play a significant pastoral role in the lives of children by caring for them and nurturing their mental and psychological growth in many ways. Fear, for example, is one of the foremost debilitating factors that hinders an individual's growth and is the cornerstone of mainstream competitive schooling in India. It has significant outcomes for relationships based on authoritarianism and privilege. Children in such schools tend to be afraid of older students and of teachers. Students with lower socio-economic or caste status are inclined to be in awe of, and simultaneously fear, the aura of privilege that may pervade an elite school. Children and young adults with disabilities of different kinds tend to fear stigma, humiliation, and the experience of being different. Teachers may also be afraid of the management, of losing their jobs, and of being out of place. All of these, and many other contexts, create an atmosphere that is completely inappropriate to the creative pedagogic, cultural, and social spaces of a learning environment. 'People who are afraid imitate others; they cling to tradition . . . and imitation destroys initiative' (Krishnamurti 1987b: 29). For creativity to awaken, 'there must be a free mind, a mind that is not burdened with tradition, with imitation' (Krishnamurti 1987b: 30). A 'free' mind is not possible when teachers compare students with one another or treat them from a position of authority and power, or when they seek to belittle their achievements.

One of the most important aspects of teacher–student relationships in a Krishnamurti school is the open quality of interaction without fear or prejudice. Such a relationship is based on an egalitarian rapport that rests on conversations and dialogue rather than on authoritarian assertions by the teacher over the student. Dialogue is at the core of Krishnamurti's approach to education. What is the actuality of 'right relationship' in a school's everyday life? Such a relationship reconfigures the pertinent dimensions of freedom, authority, and hierarchy (or the lack of these) between the students and teachers. While there is perhaps no absolute freedom in any school – and conflict is inevitable – yet dialogue, discussion, and negotiations are central to the teacher–student relationship. In the words of a former student of the Rishi Valley School, who went on to study Math at Yale, and is now a writer:

> One of the distinguishing features of schools like the one I went to is the relationship between adults and

> children. Teachers whom I knew spoke to me and treated me as though we were at the same intellectual level. You didn't feel you were in a hierarchical world, you felt you were in a world of peers that included teachers, the principal – everyone.
>
> (Sundaram 2014)

Such relationships are the basis of an ethos that constitutes school culture and is an inexorable part of a Krishnamurti school.

Krishnamurti considered education to be the means through which teachers and children could work together in an atmosphere of freedom, without fear, authority, competition, or comparison, to help understand our psychological processes as well as gain academic and technological skills. The school is in fact the centrepiece of Krishnamurti's vision for psychological development and educational excellence. It is within an educational setting that Krishnamurti hopes the seeds for individual and social change will be planted and grow through a nurturing, affectionate, and enabling environment.

Freedom in Krishnamurti's lexicon does not mean doing whatever one wants to. That is a somewhat limited and self-centred understanding of the full import of freedom. Krishnamurti emphasises that 'freedom cannot exist without order' (Krishnamurti 2016: 89) and responsibility. He refers to 'order' in the sense of 'discipline' but not in the usual meaning of the term which is to obey, conform, or imitate. He asks students to 'find out' for themselves what order is: 'you have to find out for yourself what it is to be orderly, what it is to be punctual, kind, generous, unafraid. The discovery of all that is discipline. This brings about order' (Krishnamurti 2016: 90).

For Krishnamurti, freedom and discipline go hand in hand. He says,

> Freedom cannot exist without discipline; which does not mean that you must first be disciplined and then you will have freedom. Freedom and discipline go together, they are not two separate things. So what does 'discipline' mean? According to the dictionary, the meaning

of the word 'discipline' is 'to learn' – not a mind that forces itself into a certain pattern of action according to an ideology or a belief. A mind that is capable of learning is entirely different from a mind which is capable only of conforming. A mind that is learning, that is observing, seeing actually 'what is', is not interpreting 'what is'; according to its own desires, its own conditioning, its own particular pleasures.

(Krishnamurti 1973b: 15)

Freedom, in Krishnamurti's usage, implies a mind free of any form of fear or bondage to any belief, ideology, or pattern. Such freedom carries with it the possibility of discovery, of learning without conditioning, of being open to the diversity, heterogeneity, and complexities prevalent in the human, social, and natural worlds. In other words, such a mind is free from conformity and can 'learn'.

Freedom, for Krishnamurti, does not mean being free from restraint or compulsions of any kind. That is usually what we tend to understand by the term 'being free'.

> Freedom from something is not freedom. . . . I may be rid of greed, pettiness, envy, or a dozen other things and yet not be free. . . . Freedom is a quality of the mind. That quality does not come about . . . through very careful analysis or putting ideas together.
>
> (Krishnamurti 2004: 18)

This is a freedom that emerges from the 'state and quality of the mind'. He adds, 'Without that quality, do what you will, cultivate all the virtues in the world, you will not have that freedom' (Krishnamurti 2004: 19). Freedom is therefore not about cages or prisons of different kinds from which we seek escape. 'Freedom is not in fragments' (Krishnamurti 1987a: 41). In other words, it is not about getting freedom from this, that, or the other. Contrarily, 'a non-fragmented mind, a mind that is whole, is in freedom' (Krishnamurti 1987a: 41). This has deep significance for educators working with children who, in their limited understanding, imagine or articulate freedom in its conventional sense. Teachers have to therefore rewire their own understanding of freedom and communicate this to children through their relationship with them and in their everyday encounters.

Krishnamurti also tells students that there is no utility attached to freedom: 'freedom can only exist when there is no motive' (Krishnamurti 2016: 92). It is not that one has to attain or realise something when one is free but to understand oneself, and see oneself in relationship. It is also important that one spends some time alone in order to 'find out' for oneself: 'By being with yourself, you begin to understand the workings of your own mind, and that is as important as going to class' (Krishnamurti 2016: 92). This 'seeing' of how the mind works is profound. Being free of 'one's conditioning' is the act of revolution; not to respond to either the past or what is to come, to be free of the 'habitual patterns' that one has formed over a period of time. It is then that, as Alan Kishbaugh puts it, 'one has the possibility of being free to act from no fixed position of accumulated concepts, beliefs, and perceptions' (Kishbaugh, as cited in Blau 1995: 213). Responsibility lies at the core of this freedom, not to be free from something, but instead, a sense of personal responsibility to the world; to enabling justice and peace in this tumultuous world as we know it.

Notes

1 Writing more than 20 years after India gained independence from the British, Gunnar Myrdal sums it up, *'The winning of independence has not worked any miraculous change in the people and their society'* (1968: 1649, emphasis in the original). He adds, 'The existing educational establishments are part of a larger institutional system, which includes social stratification; and this system is supported by people's attitudes, which themselves have been moulded by the institutions' (1968: 1649). This is the devastating state that Indian education finds itself in even today, more than 70 years after independence.
2 Studies have shown that children as young as four or five form strong sense of identification with their religious identity, emanating from the family, and the family's beliefs, ideas, and practices. One such conclusion is based on a study by Latika Gupta (2015)

on very young Hindu and Muslim children from an NDMC school residing in a neighbourhood of Daryaganj, a locality in Delhi. Her study reveals that children very early on show explicit identification with a particular religion and communicate prejudices towards the 'other' religion practised in their neighbourhood. They have an implicit faith in the family's religion and take pride in it. Many children refer to the family and especially the mother as having provided them with particular information about the other religion that becomes the basis for their own views. The family reinforces prevailing social attitudes and prejudices, instead of breaking them, and thereby perpetuates an exclusive religious identity that is then strengthened over time. It is therefore difficult to accept the argument that identity is natural and an instinct. It is also not an individual phenomenon in its entirety and the greater challenge lies in the contestation of the cultural and historical antecedents of identity.

3 As Neruda puts it, 'The falling wave, arch of identity, shattering feathers, is only spume when it clears, and returns to its source, unconsumed' (Neruda, *The Wide Ocean)*.
4 For a recent work on violence in a democracy like India, see Chandhoke (2021).
5 For example, see Krishna (2021). In response to Krishna, see Thapan (2021).
6 For decades now, and during Krishnamurti's lifetime as well, his work has been translated into different languages, and has reached Indians across the country. While he may have spoken and written in English, his work is available in translation as well.
7 Krishna Kumar's study of Indian and Pakistani history textbooks (Kumar 2001) is a pertinent analysis.
8 See, for example, the work of Peggy Froerer (2015) in this context.
9 Krishnamurti uses the word 'affection' more as akin to compassion.
10 See Mahmoudi et al. (2012) for a review of the holistic approach, its major proponents, and perspectives.
11 https://casel.org/what-is-sel/; (emphasis added, accessed on 18 February, 2021).
12 www.the74million.org/article/niemi-casel-is-updating-the-most-widely-recognized-definition-of-social-emotional-learning-heres-why/; (accessed on 18 February, 2021).

4

THE PRACTICE OF 'RIGHT' EDUCATION

Rishi Valley Education Centre (RVEC)

Krishnamurti's approach to education and the schools run by the KFI, some of which have been mentioned here, are of contemporary relevance for the times we live in. It is an approach that in its oldest school (a fee-paying residential school, grades 4–12) at Rishi Valley has been around for 90 years. Rishi Valley is surrounded by ancient hills, with farmers and shepherds as neighbours, where a group of concerned educators whose main task is to engage with the children in their care, work to bring about a new generation of human beings. In 1926, when J. Krishnamurti chose this piece of land, close to his birthplace, he envisioned the setting up of his first educational institution. When Krishnamurti visited the possible site (one among three) that had been earmarked for this purpose, he was struck by the presence of a large banyan tree in the Thettu valley. He wrote in a letter, 'We went round various parts and at last came across the best place. . . . I have dreamt about it twice . . . It has really a fine atmosphere' (Krishnamurti, as cited in Herzberger and Herzberger 2007: 8). Although Krishnamurti wanted 1,000 acres of land, Mr. C.S. Trilokekar went around by bullock cart, buying small pieces of land, and finally acquiring about 300 acres. It is he who named the whole basin 'Rishi Valley' (Herzberger and Herzberger 2007: 8).[1] It is recorded that Krishnamurti said about Rishi Valley, 'This is a sacred place', and S. Balasundaram, a former Principal of the Rishi Valley School, adds, it has a

> special characteristic . . . apparent to those who enter this east-west valley, one of only seven on earth, when

> they see how the valley is protected, how dense old trees canopy the roads, and people move slowly and carefully through the valley.
>
> (Balasundaram 2012: 9)[2]

From all accounts, it appears that Krishnamurti had selected the perfect place for the setting up of his first educational endeavour.

Annie Besant, who had overseen the purchase of the land for a 'world university' at Rishi Valley, soon abandoned the idea and was preoccupied with other events in the country.[3] Another school, known as the Guindy School, was started by Besant in 1918 and was based in Sadhr Gardens, Chennai (then, Madras). Its first headmaster, G.V. Subba Rao (GVS), was a young theosophist, dedicated to education. This school was run by GVS in a 'non-sectarian' manner and the presence of girl students in the school added a significant new dimension: 'Girls were admitted, first as day-scholars and later as students in residence' (Herzberger and Herzberger 2007: 13). The girls' section was inaugurated in 1923 by Besant, and she emphasised the 'importance of girls' education for the regeneration of India' (Herzberger and Herzberger 2007: 13). However, space in the Guindy School was limited, and each year the rains would cause havoc, destroying the school's thatched roofs and blowing down its cottages. After a massive cyclone in late 1930, which destroyed much of the Guindy School, Krishnamurti met GVS, and it was decided that the Guindy School would be relocated to Rishi Valley. GVS moved with approximately 90 students and their teachers. Just after this, an unprecedented 50 inches of rainfall inundated Rishi Valley's parched landscape in Rayalaseema, a drought-prone region of Andhra Pradesh. The villagers in the area considered this a blessing and a sign of prosperity.[4] This new school would now become the Rishi Valley School. In due course, the school was supplemented by a rural education centre, and a rural health centre. All of these and other resources are located as part of the Rishi Valley Education Centre (RVEC) at Rishi Valley.

Rishi Valley is located in a valley surrounded by farmers with small landholdings, and shepherds, village communities, who lead very simple lives in a somewhat arid terrain.

THE PRACTICE OF 'RIGHT' EDUCATION

Herzberger writes,

> Even those who have not been in the valley would recognise it from Krishnamurti's description – the hills that turn purple at twilight; the monsoon stream that cascades through the dry landscape, the banyan tree; the hoopoe birds bathing in the sand and the Golden Orioles with their eyes heavily outlined in black. It is a hard landscape, where poverty is writ large on the faces of the people. Ancient communities, consisting of marginal farmers and shepherds have eked out a difficult existence for five thousand years.
>
> (Herzberger n.d.b)

Krishnamurti chose this location precisely for its great natural beauty, isolation, quietude, and yet situated in the midst of the community, small farmers, shepherds, and village folk, who are the bedrock of this country. Rishi Valley is thus not an isolated community, living in a bubble, as it were. There is a mutually dependent relationship with the surroundings, environment, as well as with those who inhabit the local areas around the school. The work of the Rishi Valley Education Centre in rural education and rural health is testimony to this relationship that is sought to be nurtured with some skills, with care, affection, and resources available to the Centre.[5]

Krishnamurti's focus on inclusive education underpins Rishi Valley's rural education programme and enables us to consider individual freedom as being central to our understanding of human and social development. At the same time, the means too need to enable freedom in the very processes that engender development.[6] The Rishi Valley Education Centre in Andhra Pradesh works at the local level, with the stakeholders, with interventions that can be scaled up over a period of time. Beginning locally, with the community, and fulfilling their goals and aspirations in the most equitable manner is perhaps what makes the contribution of a civil society initiative, like that of the RVEC, imperative in the vast landscape and diverse peoplescape that constitutes India. It is in this context of building agency, among both children and teachers, in elementary school classrooms, that the Rishi Valley Institute of Educational Resources (RIVER) initiated its pedagogic method, the Multigrade-Multilevel (MGML) programme in the 1980s. The current context in which schools in this country exist is not one that is conducive to learning in the countryside. There is often one teacher in a multigrade setting. Over 92,275 schools all over India are single teacher schools (Belur 2019). This emerges out of necessity, rather than choice. Almost all such schools are government-run at the primary level, with the student strength ranging between 50 and 100. The predominant mode of teaching is through the textbook which is sacrosanct for teachers.[7] As I have pointed out elsewhere, 'the textbook is the ruler of consciousness and students emerge from their educational experience armed with knowledge but with little understanding about relationships' (Thapan 2018: 9). Teachers in most government and private schools tend to teach line by line from the textbook, and students are expected to memorise sentences and entire paragraphs to be reproduced in examinations. As a method, this reliance on textbooks fails to help children learn and induces boredom and alienation as textbooks do not often reflect the sociocultural or economic realities of students' lives. Students develop techniques and skills for rapid memorisation, and often resort to 'cheating' to pass examinations.[8] As a result, classrooms are dominated by teachers and textbooks, learning is circumscribed, and children are bored. There is little relationship between schools, parents, and the community, and the drop-out figures for children from elementary and middle school are very high.

Understanding this scenario, RIVER's Rama and Padmanabha Rao, between 1988 and 1992, developed a unique structure for elementary education at Rishi Valley that consists of a network of Satellite Schools where a community-based curriculum is taught by village youth trained in especially designed multilevel methodologies. The education kit, known as School in a Box, contains a series of carefully graded cards, replaces textbooks in the area of language, mathematics, and environmental science, and closely follows the curriculum as mandated by the National Curriculum Framework, 2005. Each card in the graded series is marked with a logo (rabbit, elephant, dog) and mapped onto a subject-specific 'Learning Ladder', a progress guide which traces out the learning trajectory for students. Spaces on the ladder are sub-divided into a set of milestones. These milestones consist of cards that explain a concept – the applications of the concept, evaluation of students' understanding and, finally, provide means of testing, remediation, or enrichment. A student identifies her own place on the ladder and creates, within the broad confines of the milestones, her own path from grade 1 to grade 5.

RIVER sees education as a tool for deepening the student's sense of herself, of her traditions and roots, while also exposing her to a wider knowledge base. This community-based model of education also incorporates ideals such as tolerance for other cultures, protection of the environment, preservation of folklore, and local medicinal traditions. Empty spaces are interspersed throughout the learning process to allow teachers to incorporate local stories, folk melodies, puzzles, nursery rhymes, and puppetry. The focus is on reviving the traditional culture so that the richness of the local culture and the teachers' own creative impulses are present and active in classrooms. At the same time, the methods encourage silent self-study and individualised learning, though teacher instruction and group work are also a necessary part of the learning process. Fast learners may progress while slower learners are allowed to work at their own pace. Students absent from school do not lose out, as they are able to start from the space in the Learning Ladder where they left off. RIVER does not want every student to be at one homogenised level ordained by textbooks with uniform content. This practice tends to iron out cultural differences and alienates a student from her own roots, and RIVER's effort has instead been to build this relationship through sustained interaction with the parents and the community.

Unfortunately, after the Right to Education (RTE) Act (2009) and new state requirements, RIVER finds itself somewhat constrained by the regulations. Several freedoms have been lost: (1) Earlier, RIVER would spread out holidays so that children were never away from school for long stretches. (2)

With the introduction of the mid-day meal, RIVER's schools are required to align working days with those of the state. (3) There is now centralised testing for older classes which means these children should study the same topics in the same order. All of these constraints have made the leeway that was earlier there in curriculum design diminish substantially (source: Interview with Dr. A. Kumaraswamy, Secretary, Rishi Valley Executive Committee).

Nonetheless, RIVER's schools have accomplished individual growth in the lap of the family and community. The agency of an individual who is able to bring about change rests on her lived experience in the family, community, and in the educational process that provides the capabilities for realising freedom/s. With adequate social opportunities, individuals can effectively shape their own destiny and help one another. Experiencing gender equality in the elementary school classroom in an atmosphere free of authoritarian culture – and so free from fear – and learning life skills is both nurturing and empowering for the fostering of freedom. RIVER's experience with the MGML method across the country and in partnership with other countries is evidence that it is possible to achieve this in great measure.

Rishi Valley School

Krishnamurti started the fee-paying school within RVEC, Rishi Valley School (RVS), with a purpose: to bring about a new generation of human beings who would be free of the conditioning of knowledge, and the past, and be able to look at life anew, in relationship to others, including nature and ideas, in an environment that was not grounded in fear or authority. He often met the senior trustees of the Krishnamurti Foundation India to discuss how he expected his schools to function. He sought commitment, dedication, responsibility, and integrity from them and the teachers in his schools to work for 'the teachings' (Krishnamurti 2017b: 3–23). Krishnamurti did not however offer a blueprint or guidelines on how to do this and left it to the trustees, senior administrators and teachers to implement his educational vision.

In the long years of its existence, Rishi Valley School has seen many administrative shifts and changes in the way Krishnamurti's vision has been understood, incorporated, and practised at school. Different people at the helm of affairs have brought their own experience, initiative, and perspective to enrich Krishnamurti's rich legacy. Krishnamurti is not an explicit presence at the school; he passed away in 1986, and with that ended his annual visits to the school when he spoke to teachers and students, expressing his views with passion and engaging in dialogue with many different stakeholders including trustees, teachers, and students. His views inform school values and many practices, but there is no single ideological framework within which these may be found. Herzberger has noted, 'We try to put values in the curriculum that have come out of Krishnamurti's teachings, like the love of peace, the love of nature, the relationship between human beings and the environment' (Herzberger, as cited in Kuyper 2014; 48). These and other values are shared across the spectrum of what a Krishnamurti school is (not, *should be*) and yet, Krishnamurti's principles have been steadfastly adhered to. In a sense, there have been variations on the theme that Krishnamurti expressed and yet, certain constants remain. I consider these central to life at Rishi Valley and examine them here as three fluid, interactive, and interdependent aspects of the educational process at RVS.[9] These are critical to developing a moral intelligence that is essential for the well-being and sustenance of the world and may be understood as relationship, school culture, and equity and social justice.

a) Relationship

When Krishnamurti visited Rishi Valley in 1979, he asked a gathering of teachers and students about the purpose of education. Herzberger tells us,

> He claimed that by 'cultivating' a very narrow area of the mind, that part which is connected with memorising information, teachers, even though they might not realise it, are impoverishing the soil in which students grow

and are in turn betraying their true calling. . . . The word [cultivate] comes from a Latin root, he said, meaning 'to take care', 'to worship', 'to have tremendous respect'. For Krishnamurti these emotionally tinged concerns define the teachers' relationship with their students, and underpin the ultimate purposes of education.

(Herzberger 2011: 1)

F.G. Pearce (1892–1961), who served as the Principal of the Rishi Valley School from 1950–1958, was quick to understand that this emphasis on relationship was the leitmotif of Krishnamurti's educational thought. He notes,

the experiment in relationship now being carried out at Rishi Valley has enabled me to see more clearly, even in the last few months I have been here, . . . that there is no life without relationship, and that relationship is the only mirror in which we can know ourselves and thereby come to know others.
(Pearce, as cited in Krishnan and Krishnan 2017: 49)

Relationship is the *sine qua non* of school life: to relate to people, to ideas, to nature, and to everything around us. Understanding the breadth and depth of Krishnamurti's assertion 'you are the world' brings about a tremendous sense of responsibility as participants engage in living and learning together in an educational setting. This responsibility is not only concerned with our 'petty little worlds', as Krishnamurti often said, but also about the whole existence of life. 'To be is to be related', is another of Krishnamurti's oft-quoted statements. We do not exist in isolation and when we understand this, not merely intellectually or theoretically, but viscerally, with a sense of conscious awareness, we can never experience ourselves as only an individual in a bounded or enclosed space that is ours alone. This requires an understanding that we need to stretch ourselves outside our known universe of comfort and privilege, our closed circle of friends or clique of intimate friends, to understand the lives and experience of others who may be less privileged, have no access to education or livelihood opportunities, who may speak a different language, or have a special faith, a unique life story, and so on.

In an educational setting, relationship affects the nature of communication between participants in the schooling process, especially between students and teachers. If there is an authoritarian relationship, bound by fear and anxiety, there is weak communication, and students are unable to connect to teachers except in a very formal sense. The relationship therefore has to overcome this separation and allow a process of 'intimate communication' to unfold in the context of everyday life in an institutional setting. Sonkar, who has focused her study of the Rishi Valley School on this aspect of the school's life, emphasises that 'the relationship between a teacher and her students is a delicate relationship composed on the dimensions of freedom, order, and hierarchy'. Citing Krishnamurti, she concludes, 'It is not the presence of these dimensions, but their "*unorchestrated absence*" that are necessary to strengthen the bond' (Krishnamurti, as cited in Sonkar 2018: 148, emphasis in the original) between teachers and students.

In an earlier work, I delineated the presence of two orders in the school: the transcendental and local orders (Thapan 2006: 28ff). I examined the 'transcendental order' as being concerned 'essentially with values and the production of a new kind of human being through the process of self-knowledge and transformation'. Through this, I attempted to describe Krishnamurti's world view as a significant scaffolding for the transcendental order that laid out the intentions and goals of the school. I distinguished this from the school's 'local order' which is based on 'the school as an institution and is mainly concerned with the reproduction of knowledge through the transmission of educational knowledge' (Thapan 2006: 28). In other words, this order seemed to be concerned with actual schooling processes and the educational practices contained therein. At the time, I considered these two orders as separate and not necessarily in sync with one another. The local order often appeared to contradict many of the aims of the transcendental order and was thus not in harmony with Krishnamurti's educational perspective. However, I must emphasise that my continued association with the school has in fact showed me how the transcendental and local orders go hand in hand and function together in an intermeshed and interdependent manner. This may give rise to conflict at times not only with Krishnamurti's thought but also in the everyday functioning of the school. At times, boundaries have to be set for student behaviour, for teacher articulations, as well as spatial markers, and for so many other aspects of school life. There are also certain expectations about student behaviour, which may appear to suggest that students have very little 'freedom' while they are in school. For example, while there is no school uniform, sartorial choices are not left completely open and students are expected to adhere to some kind of decorum which is stated in the school Handbook sent to parents each year. Similarly, the school practices a vegetarian policy in the dining hall which may once again suggest that free choice is being curtailed. The school routine with fixed timings for classes, sport, meals, and other activities is indicative of a structured and inflexible routine. This is not always the case and often there are modifications to the school day based on special events or activities. There are some aspects of school life that are indeed non-negotiable, and these include a rigorous academic programme and pedagogies that enable learning in an environment free of fear, comparison, competition, and excessive control.

It is important to note that Krishnamurti was not against academic work, and in fact, sought academic excellence in his schools. At the same time, he was concerned about the student's psychological development and emphasised the need for the two to be in tandem, in continuous harmony for holistic education to prevail. What is important is how this coming together of the transcendental and the local takes place. This depends on the 'relationships' between different functionaries and between teachers and students. To establish, nurture, and sustain such relationships lies at the heart of the school culture which is made up of the participants in school and the life they breathe into its everyday functioning.

A congenial and close relationship between teachers and students is encouraged and is dependent on the openness with which the teachers approach all kinds of students with their idiosyncrasies and ideas not only about teachers but also about themselves, one another, and the world. Such relationships therefore rest on the bonds that teachers are able to establish with students, in a residential school, with the children in their pastoral care. Through conversations and concerns raised in the 'houses' where they live together and through the many informal spaces they occupy in the school, a spirit of 'intimate communication' reflects the ideal state of such communication, or what Samdhong Rinpoche stated as 'compassionate communication', on his visit to Rishi Valley in 2016. This is the perfect state that must prevail in order for the bond to develop between teachers and students. This is not always possible as teachers come from diverse social backgrounds with a variety of interests and commitments. Not all teachers are necessarily cued into Krishnamurti's educational vision although there are regular weekly teacher meetings to share, discuss, and examine aspects of Krishnamurti's work. There is no official policy or 'method' as such through which this relationship is sought to be established. Krishnamurti's approach allows educators the space and initiative through which they may seek to engage with the children in different ways to establish 'right' relationship. Thus, each relationship develops through interaction, openness, a spirit of dialogue and engagement based on how teachers seek to develop and sustain such relationships. Sonkar notes,

> In its illustrious history, RVS has received teachers who have often engaged with Krishnamurti's philosophy in one way or the other. They might have disagreed with it, but they would engage with it in talks and dialogue. There have also been teachers who 'heard' about Krishnamurti when they first came to RVS. This has resulted in a multiplicity of voice and agency as it is the teachers who bring in their diverse perspectives in the absence of an official view on right relationship.
> (Sonkar 2018: 156)

It is also the case that, on arrival at RVS, new teachers often find the situation somewhat alarming due to the culture of informality and freedom that prevails in the school. It is with some time that they begin to understand that students and teachers actually face a very good rapport (Sonkar 2018: 157). What may appear at first as 'indiscipline' in fact helps in understanding problems and in shaping the classroom encounter and interaction in the house as well.

There is also a diversity in the student population who come from backgrounds where the choice of school rests merely on its reputation as being among the top residential co-educational schools in India. There are others who studied at RVS themselves or are looking for an 'alternative school' for their children's education. Krishnamurti continuously emphasised the role of parents in their children's education and reiterated that education is a joint project, dependent on parents as much as on educators. Undoubtedly, in a residential school, parents are usually absent except for short periods when they visit the school. The everyday life of the institution is therefore supported by those closest to the children, their teachers, administrators, and workers in the school. They work together to provide a culture that children remember years after they have graduated from school. Children themselves bring their perspectives, actions, and behaviour to this space, creating meaning and giving life to an institution that would actually be bereft of life if it was not for their presence. This coming together of different persona in one space, to partake of a process that is about learning together and living together, is what creates the culture of the school. Schools are spaces where such school culture prevails and is an inevitable part of everyday life.

b) School Culture

School culture is not a concrete aspect of school life. It is an atmosphere that is created by the teachers and enriched by students through their presence, their engagement with school processes and with all aspects of school life. It is not, however, a simple task: to create this atmosphere. It has to be worked at, built brick by brick, in the penumbra of everyday school life. Such a culture rests on how teachers and students interact with one another and among themselves to ensure that the 'atmosphere' exists, permeates all aspects of their life at school, and perpetuates itself. It is not an ideal state, devoid of challenges or conflict, and this further presents itself as what being at school is all about. Working together, across age and linguistic differences, aspirations or goals, difficulties, and problems, is essential for the culture to be sustained through time. However, all school cultures are not unique and often remain embedded in the material and complex structures of everyday life. It is the Krishnamurti schools that hold out the promise of a nuanced school culture enhanced by the quality of relationships and interactions that endure within.

Pearce wrote in a letter (in 1956) to his friends in Sri Lanka,

> This year we seem to have reached the point of seeing clearly that the first and all important essential of 'the right kind of education' is the right kind of atmosphere in which the children feel at home, and in which alone they can develop intelligence and creativity.
> (Pearce, as cited in Krishnan and Krishnan 2017: 118)

He considered it essential to the task of holistic education that Krishnamurti espoused. Rishi Valley at his time was enthused with an atmosphere of freedom, academic excellence and several activities that enriched the life of the community (Herzberger and Herzberger 2007). One activity that contributed significantly to school culture was *astachal* (lit., the place where the sun sets) that Pearce initiated and continues in the present day. Children and teachers watch the sunset together at a particular spot establishing a quality of silence, reflection, and quietude. This ensures a particular dimension to the school culture that is significant, that of leisure. Students appreciate this quality, and the spot itself acquires a sacred dimension in their memory.[10] When former students visit the valley, they walk up to the *astachal* and relive their experience as they do when they visit other favourite spots on campus. In an interview, Herzberger has emphasised this aspect of the school culture:

> Something rubs off on the children and that is more important than talking and preaching. I feel that this is the most important thing: to be quiet, to be quiet

yourself and communicate this somewhat, to communicate some quietness instead of all those words. You get lost in words and children do not really understand. Giving them affection, something positive, is always better.
(Herzberger, as cited in Kuyper 2014: 43)

Herzberger practices quiet periods of silence in her culture classes with students each week. Students do not rebel and quietly undertake the exercise. School culture is made up of this atmosphere of quietude that communicates itself to children and adults alike. The natural beauty of the valley is another feature that adds to the quality of stillness and silence that communicates itself to children.

School ethos or culture is not made up of the trivia of school life. As educators, we often imagine that it is and therefore pay so much attention to the detail of the routine, the schedule, the manner in which we keep children, and ourselves, occupied throughout the day. More than the school routine and the everyday academic life of the institution, school culture is a process. How then, do we define this process? What is this ethos, this culture, that prevails in an educational setting that is not about academic scholarship alone, that liberates even as it circumscribes, that helps one to push one's boundaries as a teacher, and as children, that enables a rich understanding of the multidimensional facets of life, and simultaneously expects one to be 'good' at what one does. Krishnamurti did not accept mediocrity as a virtue in the same way as he did not cherish the burden of memory, which is embodied in knowledge, which we worship, as representative of truth. Instead, he asked us to look, to listen, and to learn, as if we were doing it for the first time, in other words, to be fresh in our approach to learning. There would in this way never be a mere accumulation of knowledge or the regurgitation of what may be considered legitimate knowledge, but an understanding that comes with intelligence, empathy, and compassion.

School culture is not grounded only in a rush of activities, the routine school day. It is based on the relationships within school and those that teachers, children, parents, and the community bring to the school. In the flurry of activities, sports, theatre, art, and music that mark a regular school day, school culture in a Krishnamurti school is also marked by stillness. The morning assembly and evening *astachal* are two acts that seek to instil stillness as integral aspects of the everyday. By posting them in the routine, they are interwoven into the fabric of school life and are a part of the process of learning that constitutes schooling. The quality of stillness that quietens the mind and allows the space with which one can listen with a fresh mind, as it were, is essential for not only children but also teachers who are often burdened with the trivia of routine. It is in such an atmosphere that learning takes places, based on trust and mutual affection. As teachers and students, it is important to be attentive to this atmosphere, that Krishnamurti has brought to this school in the beginning and which has been experienced by so many others.

At the same time, for such a culture to flourish, we must understand ourselves and others as mutually interdependent human beings in relationship to one another and to the world we inhabit. This involves bringing about an expanded idea of the individual to children in the everyday life of an educational setting. Pushing out the boundaries of the self is not unimaginable or impossible. With time, children may come to understand that it is possible to see the other who may look different, or belong to another community or caste, as part of a larger inclusive whole in which we are all connected as a disparate but collective entity. This is possible only if we allow children to actually ask questions about issues of identity and respond to them equally honestly. Identity is not a fixed idea or experience. It is in movement; it is fluid: I experience as many aspects of myself at the intersection of multiple facets of being a person as does everyone else. The space for dialogue in everyday life requires a culture that is open to questioning, to honest conversations about ourselves and others, to explore nuances of relationships that are often unexpressed or remain outside the field of formal education, per se. This once again comes down to school culture, and to maintaining an ethos that is conducive to such conversations and to enabling a more non-violent and just social world.

c) Equity and Social Justice

As a proponent of world peace, Krishnamurti was well aware of the inequities in society and, as earlier mentioned, used to ask students and teachers at his schools if they were even aware of the life of the community in which they were embedded, and of the inequalities and misery outside the school. He did not want children to experience their lives in a protected bubble at school and outside. Being part of the world is an essential part of growing up at a Krishnamurti school. At the same time, bringing inclusivity and diversity into school life cannot be an ideological or mechanical enterprise. It needs to be built into the school culture, become an inextricable part of it, and thereby enrich the consciousness of educators and students alike. It is also important to ensure that only one aspect of social injustice is not represented, examined, or understood, at the cost of other equally violent acts of social trauma and injustice. Intersectionality is a buzzword in contemporary academic and activist circles and needs to be understood in the context of school culture. It is imperative to understand, following Carbado, Crenshaw, Mays, and Tomlinson, that intersectionality is a 'disposition' as much as it is a method, a 'heuristic and analytical tool' (2013: 303). Caste, class, religion, and gender inequities are perhaps not all experienced with the same intensity in a Krishnamurti school. Children and young adults tend to see their immediate and most intimate experience and social world as one that frames the entire universe. It is through 'culture' classes and assembly talks that the school seeks to build the experience of going beyond the self and seeing the larger world that may lie outside one's own lived experience. This is done through discussion around caste, gender, religion, class, and other forms of group identities including language, terrain, and nationality, to see how they intersect and exclude other ways of looking at the world. This is done with the conscious intent to view the world through an open and expanded lens that takes account of other experiences, and lived realities. The presence of Saturday clubs including those such as 'current affairs' or 'understanding contemporary India' in the curriculum also serves to foreground social challenges pertaining to equity and social justice in the lives of students who may belong to largely privileged socio-economic backgrounds.

An engagement with the work of the rural education centre at Rishi Valley is another area which children are encouraged to partake of. The MGML pedagogic method that is the hallmark of the Rishi Valley Education Centre has been implemented in its mathematics programme at the elementary level in RVS as well. This has enhanced learning outcomes in different ways and draws attention to the work of the rural education centre in diverse settings. There is mutual cooperation and engagement between the rural education centre and RVS.

Children of the seventh grade have an exchange programme with children in the rural middle school whom they meet every week to learn from them and also to 'teach' them some dimension of school work. It could be language teaching, an exchange of English and Telugu skills, or some other aspect of school life. Some senior school students are engaged with the work of the rural health centre through projects in subject areas such as Biology. Through this, they not only begin to understand the outreach programmes of the school but also engage with the community, understand the difficulties and anxieties of the community, and work towards ameliorating some of them.

It is a complex and difficult task: to bring about an awareness, sensitivity, and empathy for disadvantaged and marginalised sections of society and simultaneously to help children understand the urgency with which this needs to be corrected. It is even more difficult for young people to comprehend at some depth that we need to examine ourselves and our lives first: are we discriminatory in our approach towards others? How do we experience 'difference' in our everyday relations with one another and with society? Can we watch our own behaviour, seek to expand our understanding and correct ourselves? These are some of the questions that teachers seek to work with in this context. It is not possible, however, to evaluate the extent to which students develop an awareness and sensitivity to such issues or a commitment to bringing about social justice. This is only unravelled in the lives they lead once they leave school and become part of an expanded and diverse social network and public life.

Notes

1 Mr. Trilokekar was a member of the Theosophical Society.
2 In recent times, Samdhong Rinpoche visited Rishi Valley and declared 'the atmosphere completely different' from that at any other KFI school (2016, personal conversation).
3 Annie Besant was now deeply involved with the 'Home Rule League' movement that she was in fact leading and with national politics in India.
4 Rishi Valley was declared a Special Development Area (RVSDA) by the Government of Andhra Pradesh in 2008 and constitutes the Rishi Valley Special Development Authority (RVSDA). The primary task of this initiative is to 'protect and conserve Rishi Valley's ecological diversity and prevent it from being degraded, through unrestrained growth; ensure conservation that does not compromise the livelihoods of rural communities of the area and ensures inclusive growth of all stakeholders; and preserve Rishi Valley's cultural heritage' (source: www.rishivalley.org/special-development-area).
5 See www.rishivalley.org, www.rishivallyrec.org for further details. Krishnamurti's work must be understood from the entire vision that he provided impacting education not only for the fee-paying schools but also for the work for rural education done by the Krishnamurti Foundation India. The Multigrade-Multilevel (MGML) pedagogic method envisioned by the Rishi Valley Rural Education Centre has been adapted and is being used in more than 250,000 elementary schools in India and in several countries including Nepal, Kenya, and Sri Lanka. More than 125 million students in India have been impacted by this methodology, and the effort is to extend this to many other schools in remote areas of the country where children have little or no access to education. Teacher training in this methodology has benefitted almost 12,000 master trainers or facilitators around the country, and bi-annual teacher training courses on Krishnamurti's approach to education are part of the work of the Foundation.
6 Sen (1999) has persuasively argued that 'Freedoms are not only the primary ends of development; they are also among its principal means'. In other words, the processes through which we seek to bring about development must reflect the intent of development.
7 See Krishna Kumar (2015) on the relationship between texts and values, Dipti Bhog et al. (2015), and more recently, Pooja Bhalla (2017) on different aspects of the textbook culture in India.
8 Bhalla (2017) focuses on this aspect of school culture. She considers cheating a pedagogic device that students use to fulfil their objective of passing the examination.

9 I am well aware that there are other aspects of school life at Rishi Valley that merit close attention but for purposes of this work, I focus on these three alone in the interest of parsimony and space.
10 See Thapan (2006) for students' accounts of their experience at *astachal*.

5
CHALLENGES AND CONTINUITIES

Krishnamurti's educational vision is a challenge not just in the context of the educational scenario in this country where the textbook is dominant, and teachers are authoritarian and assertive, and schools are spaces that lack the sensitivity and intellectual breadth with which to approach education in the twenty-first century. It is an enormous task to sustain the quality of care and attention that children and young adults demand in a learning environment. There is a need for commitment, and a steadfastness of goals that can steer the schools in Krishnamurti's direction and can nurture the atmosphere, the school culture, and other resources that are essential to a Krishnamurti school. In each school, therefore, there is a core group of resource persons who have been associated with one or another Krishnamurti school in teaching or administrative capacities and move around the schools helping in this process, often spending long periods of time at different Krishnamurti schools in India. They provide the direction and quality of attention that an engagement with Krishnamurti's thought requires in everyday school practice. The 'modern' world with all its entanglements can easily distract from the essential principles that are central to 'right' education, and there is a need therefore to have continuous debate, discussion, and share ideas and practices among the practitioners between the different Krishnamurti schools in India. Teachers from these schools meet annually at a teachers' conference held over a few days at one of the schools. This is usually on a particular theme and is meant for all teachers from the schools. In recent years, a core group of educators, under the leadership of a senior trustee of the Krishnamurti Foundation India, has started a teacher education programme 'The Role of a Teacher' based exclusively on Krishnamurti's educational vision and school practices. The programme is for a period of four months usually with an immersion in two of the Krishnamurti schools for a period of two weeks for each participant.[1]

Despite these interventions and the continuous engagement with innovative ideas about pedagogy, teacher quality, curriculum development, pastoral care, and many other dimensions of school life, there are some aspects that continue to challenge teachers in Krishnamurti schools. The onslaught of media on young minds, especially frequent use of social media and free access to different kinds of online platforms, takes a toll on children's understanding of themselves, on their relations with one another and very importantly on their mental health. Student explorations of their identities and their engagement with one another in this context, where one set of students feels marginalised and excluded, and others feel uncomfortable with alternative student views, raise serious concerns for teachers and administrators. Social media is consumed by questions about 'identity' in one way or another, and this impacts young minds deeply. Engaging with these posts on social media in an excessive or obsessive manner may result in students questioning their own identities and those of their peers and older generations. A divide is created which adds to already existing schisms that may exist in any institution, despite its efforts to address such cleavages.

The prevailing socio-economic crises and the varied outcomes of the COVID-19 pandemic have contributed to creating an increasingly bleak atmosphere in which education in India is already embedded. There has been an overwhelming reliance on online education in the pandemic which has in turn excluded large sections of the young population. According to the National Sample Survey Report on Education (2017–2018), only 24 per cent of Indian households have an internet facility. While 66 per cent of India's population lives in villages, only a little over 15 per cent of rural households have access to internet services. For urban households, the proportion is 42 per cent. In fact, only 8 per cent of all households with members aged between 5 and 24 have both a computer and an internet connection.[2] These abysmal figures emphasise the inaccessibility of educational resources to the large mass of people in the country. Apart from the digital divide created by this mode of delivery, and its pedagogic consequences, for both teachers and students, lack of access has resulted in some students taking their lives due to their inability to participate. When such a dire situation prevails, education for peace is far from the minds of educators who have been grappling with changes and uncertainties due to the vagaries of the pandemic. This is the context in which India finds itself as it struggles to emerge from the aftermath of the pandemic.

In dealing with the extraordinary crises that have been triggered by the pandemic, a set of important questions emerge for our consideration as educators in India. These questions are concerned with issues such as the educational experience of mobile children during the pandemic, for example, of the Bakarwal and Gujjar communities in Kashmir, or children of migrants who move between their villages and the cities in search of livelihoods.

We also need to understand the fate of children who are differently abled and their experience during the pandemic. The hearing and speech impaired would have had a different involvement with online education. Similarly, the situation of out-of-school girl children in states like Bihar and Rajasthan needs to be carefully unravelled. Are they at work, have they been sucked into child marriages? What are their educational aspirations post-pandemic?

Above all, the impact of the demands for online education on our understanding of education as it is practiced, in terms of curricula, pedagogy, social, and human interaction need to be understood as does the fate of children who are deprived of contact with other children for long periods of time. The question educators need to urgently address grapples with the possibilities of challenging and changing the imperatives imposed by the pandemic and working towards an educational scenario where justice, equity, and peace prevail in equal measure.

Krishnamurti's voice for a distinctive education, geared towards self-inquiry and a concern for humanity and the environment, has been echoed in the work of other scholars and organisations. Brian Jenkins, who taught for several years at Brockwood Park school (run by the Krishnamurti Foundation Trust, UK), started the Sholai school in the Palani hills, Kodaikanal, in 1989. Inspired by Krishnamurti's thought, the school has a focus on creating an atmosphere in which 'children are encouraged to enjoy learning and to grow to be mature and sensitive individuals' (school website).[3] The school, set in 35 acres of land in a larger estate of 100 acres, has a holistic approach to education, paying attention to the physical and emotional well-being of students in addition to their intellectual development. A former student writing on his experience at the school says,

> In the last few years I've become aware of a lot more things and their importance, such as: learning about myself and my relationships; the employment that the school provides to the nearby villagers and trying to be selfless and consume less and give equally back to nature. Sholai provides chances to live a better life that is sustainable, eco-friendly and where one learns about oneself. Though these may not seem like very much, contemplating on it, one understands the significance and importance of them.
>
> (school website)

Such an honest testimonial speaks volumes for the kind of education the school offers and the nurturance it provides to the children in its care.

The Centre for Learning (CFL) in Bengaluru was started by a group of concerned individuals in 1990 and has also been inspired by Krishnamurti's educational vision (school website).[4] It is a small school with only about 70 children and works with them in modest classes, paying individual attention, and helping children understand their emotions, as well as, paying attention to their physical and intellectual growth. It describes itself on the school website:

> CFL is a community of students and adults interested in learning about ourselves and our relationship with the world. This learning involves not only academics and other life skills, but also a deeper exploration about our emotions and thought processes and the way we respond to the challenges of life. The questions raised by J Krishnamurti play a significant role in our educational vision.
>
> (school website)

Another small school in Bengaluru, Shibumi, has also been inspired by Krishnamurti's educational vision and defines itself 'not a community that one joins. It is a coming together of individuals, in the spirit of freedom and cooperation, in the movement of self-knowing through dialogue and observation' (school website).[5]

At the same time, apart from the Krishnamurti Foundation India and these like-minded schools, there are others, trusts, and non-governmental organisations who have initiated work in the field of school education. The Nobel laureate, Tenzin Gyatso, the 14th Dalai Lama, has for some years now been promoting his vision of 'universal ethics' in school curricula. He uses the Tibetan word *kun long* (lit. 'from the depths') as being understood as 'what drives or inspires our actions – both those we intend directly and those which are in a sense involuntary. It therefore denotes the individual's overall state of heart and mind' (Dalai Lama 2000: 31). Akin to Krishnamurti's use of 'thought-feeling', the Dalai Lama suggests that the Tibetan word for mind is *lo* 'which includes the ideas of feeling and emotion (heart) alongside those of consciousness, or awareness' (Dalai Lama 2000: 31). In other words, emotions and thoughts are not divisible and together shape our behaviour. Based on the Buddhist concept of 'dependent origination', the Dalai Lama emphasises the 'interdependence' of all phenomena which implies the interconnectedness between not just humans but between humans and nature, the earth, and everything. There is a wholeness to consciousness which is inclusive, not separated by class, religion, language, gender, or any other category of separation. There is in fact 'a complex interlinking of relationships' and even the identity of the 'self' does 'not denote an independent object. Rather it is a label we apply to a complex web of interrelated phenomena' (Dalai Lama 2000: 41–42). This, the Dalai Lama believes, results in the 'recognition of our *shared humanity*' and of '*interdependence* as a key feature of human reality' (Dalai Lama 2011: 19, emphasis in the original).[6] Increasingly, 'modern education', as the Dalai Lama puts it, emphasises only academic learning and neglects to pay attention to emotions which together form the basis of our action. This results in a kind of lopsided education. He thus emphasises the need for an education that lays equal emphasis on all aspects of growing up so that the seeds are sown for ethical behaviour. The Dalai Lama's concern has been shaped and developed by Emory University's Social, Emotional, and Ethical (SEE) Learning programme for children in primary through high school[7]. Based on the Dalai Lama's vision, a non-governmental organisation in Delhi, Ayur Gyan Nyas (AGN) seeks to change the educational landscape by bringing in values that resonate with developing a global outlook, empathy and compassion for others, and a holistic education. AGN has developed curricula on four dimensions of 'Universal Ethics' so as to 'help students to regulate his/her emotions and behaviour, ultimately making them happier, healthier, academically competent and more adept in facing the challenges of the modern world'. AGN works with different schools all over India, training teachers, introducing their curriculum, helping in developing an understanding of their main ideas and resource material, and creating an atmosphere where teachers and the schools seek to practice the curriculum and the activities associated with it.[8]

There is no doubt that Krishnamurti's educational perspective has inspired educators not only in India but also in other parts of the world where schools have been started for young children. None of these schools, or those run by the Krishnamurti

Foundations in India, the United Kingdom, and the United States, claim to be completely successful in carrying out Krishnamurti's vision. Krishnamurti's educational endeavour is in process and still unfolding in the schools established by him. Each school is unique and carries its own particular process and practice forward depending on a variety of factors, most importantly, the participants who are engaged with Krishnamurti and his vision. It is no doubt also an encounter that carries with it challenges, imperatives, and continuities that serve to underline the unique dimensions of an educational experience that aims to bring about peace and social transformation.

Notes

1 During the COVID-19 pandemic, the school immersion has not been possible but the course has nonetheless been running on schedule.
2 http://mospi.nic.in/sites/default/files/publication_reports/KI_Education_75th_Final.pdf (accessed on 4 August, 2021).
3 www.sholaicloaat.org/v2/ (accessed on 2 September, 2021).
4 https://cfl.in/ (accessed on 2 September, 2021).
5 https://www.shibumi.org.in/ (accessed on 2 September, 2021).
6 Due to the paucity of space, I have portrayed the Dalai Lama's work on universal ethics and secular education in a brief, simplistic manner. For fuller accounts of his perspective, please see Dalai Lama (2000, 2011), Aguilar (2021), among others.
7 For more details about this remarkable program and its implementation around the world, please see https://seelearning.emory.edu/ (accessed on 2 September, 2021).
8 See https://ayurgyannyas.org for more details about their mission and work in different states in India. See also Gulati (2021).

REFERENCES

Aguilar, Mario. 2021. *The 14th Dalai Lama: Peacekeeping and Universal Responsibility*. Routledge, Taylor and Francis Series on Peacemakers (ed. Ramin Jahanbegloo). New York and London, Routledge, Taylor and Francis.

Althusser, Louis. 1971. Ideology and Ideological State Apparatuses. (Notes towards an Investigation.) In *Lenin and Philosophy and Other Essays*. New York, Monthly Review Press.

Arendt, Hannah. 2006. *Eichmann in Jerusalem. A Report on the Banality of Evil*. Penguin Classics. www.goodreads.com/quotes/405900-adolf-eichmann-went-to-the-gallows-with-great-dignity-he (accessed on 16 June, 2021).

Balasundaram, S. 2012. *Non-Guru Guru. My Years with J. Krishnamurti* (eds. R.E. Mark Lee and M.V. Prasad). Ojai, Edwin House Publishing, Inc.

Belur, Rashmi. 2019. Single Teacher Schools. Karnataka Ranks #6 in India with 4700 Such Schools. www.edexlive.com/news/2019/jan/23/single-teacher-schools-ktaka-ranks-6-in-india-with-4700-such-schools-5123.html (accessed on 7 September, 2021).

Bhalla, Pooja. 2017. *Implementation of New Textbooks: A Study of Elementary Classroom Processes in a Kendriya Vidyalaya in Delhi*. Unpublished Doctoral Thesis, University of Delhi.

Bhog, Dipta et al. 2015. Plotting the Contours of the Modern Nation. A Feminist Reading of Geography Textbooks. In Meenakshi Thapan (ed.) *Education and Society. Themes, Perspectives, Practices*. Oxford in India Readings in Sociology and Social Anthropology. New Delhi, Oxford University Press. Pp. 358–378.

Blau, Evelyne. 1995. *Krishnamurti. 100 Years*. New York, Stewart, Tabori & Chang. A Joost Elffers Book.

REFERENCES

Blavatsky, H.P. 1962. *The Secret Doctrine*. Madras, Theosophical Publishing House.
———. 1972. *Isis Unveiled*. Pasadena, Theosophical University Press.
———. 1987. *Key to Theosophy*. London, Theosophical Publishing House.
Bourdieu, Pierre. 1977. *Outline of a Theory of Practice*. Cambridge, Polity Press.
Bourdieu, Pierre, and J.C. Passeron. 1977. *Reproduction in Education, Society and Culture*. London, Sage Publications.
Carbado, Devon W., Kimberlé Williams Crenshaw, Vickie M. Mays, and Barbara Tomlinson. 2013. Intersectionality. Mapping the Movements of a Theory. *Du Bois Review of Social Science Research on Race*, Volume 10, Issue 2: Pp. 303–312.
Carnoy, Martin. 1974. *Education as Cultural Imperialism*. New York, Longman, Inc.
Chandhoke, Neera. 2021. *The Violence in Our Bones: Mapping the Deadly Fault Lines Within Indian Society*. New Delhi, Aleph Book Company.
Chandmal, Asit. 1985. *One Thousand Moons: Krishnamurti at Eighty-Five*. New York, Harry N. Abrams, Inc.
Dalai Lama, His Holiness. 2000. *Ancient Wisdom, Modern World. Ethics for the New Millennium*. London, Abacus.
——— 2011. *Beyond Religion. Ethics for a Whole World*. New York, Houghton Mifflin Harcourt.
Dharampal. 2000. (1983). *Collected Writings. Vol III. The Beautiful Tree. Indigenous Indian Education in the Eighteenth Century*. Mapusa, Other India Press.
Friere, Paulo. 2005. (1970). *Pedagogy of the Oppressed*. Translated by Myra B. Ramos. New York and London, Continuum.
Froerer, Peggy. 2015. Disciplining the Saffron Way. Moral Education and the Hindu *Rashtra*. In Meenakshi Thapan (ed.) *Education and Society. Themes, Perspectives, Practices*. Oxford in India Readings in Sociology and Social Anthropology. New Delhi, Oxford University Press. Pp. 221–260.
Gandhi, M.K. 1909. (1997). *Hind Swaraj and Other Writings*. Translated by Anthony J. Parel. New Delhi, Cambridge University Press India Pvt. Ltd.
Gulati, Deeksha. 2021. Educating Heart and Mind: Imparting Universal Ethics Education in Schools in India. www.dpublication.com/wp-content/uploads/2021/02/106-816.pdf (accessed on 8 September, 2021).

REFERENCES

Gupta, Latika. 2015. Formation of Religious Identity in Early Childhood. In Meenakshi Thapan (ed.) *Education and Society. Themes, Perspectives, Practices*. Oxford in India Readings in Sociology and Social Anthropology. New Delhi, Oxford University Press. Pp. 191–211.

Herzberger, Hans and Radhika Herzberger. 2007. *Rishi Valley School. The First Forty Years*. Rishi Valley, Krishnamurti Foundation India and Rishi Valley Education Centre.

Herzberger, Radhika. n.d.a. *An Overview of J. Krishnamurti's Writings on Education*. Unpublished paper. (Personal hard copy).

———. n.d.b. *J. Krishnamurti's Legacy*. Unpublished paper. (Personal hard copy).

———. 1999. Education and Indian Nationalism. *Journal of the Krishnamurti Schools*, Issue 3. http://journal.kfionline.org/issue-3 (accessed on 8 May, 2021).

———. 2011. Introduction, *Krishnamurti Foundation India Bulletin*, Volume 9, Issue 1, November 2011–February 2012: Pp. 1–2.

———. 2015. Private Virtue and Public Space. Education in a Fragile World. In Meenakshi Thapan (ed.) *Education and Society. Themes, Perspectives, Practices*. Oxford in India Readings in Sociology and Social Anthropology. New Delhi, Oxford University Press. Pp. 98–117.

Jayakar, Pupul. 1987. *J. Krishnamurti. A Biography*. Calcutta, Penguin Books.

Kakar, Sudhir. 1981. *The Inner World. A Psycho-Analytic Study of Childhood and Society in India*. New Delhi, Oxford University Press.

Kaplan, Robert D. 1996. *The Ends of the Earth. A Journey to the Frontiers of Anarchy*. New York, Vintage Books.

Krishna, T.M. 2021. The Silences of Jiddu Krishnamurti. www.theindiaforum.in/article/silences-jiddu-krishnamurti (accessed on 16 May, 2021).

Krishnamurti, J. 1912. *Education as Service*. Chicago, The Rajput Press. www.fulltextarchive.com/page/Education-as-Service/ (accessed on 23 April, 2021).

———. 1929. Speech Dissolving the Order of the Star. August 3, 1929. https://sites.google.com/site/lamaisonkrishnamurticentre/Krishnamurti/speech-on-dissolving-the-order-of-the-star (accessed on 28 April, 2021).

———. 1945. Ojai 2nd Public Talk 1945. Jkrishnamurti.org/nl/content/ojai-2nd-public-talk-1945 (accessed on 31 January, 2022).

REFERENCES

———.1948. The 6th Public Talk, Poona, October 3, 1948. https://jkrishnamurti.org/content/poona-india-6th-public-talk-3rd-october-1948 (accessed on 6 June, 2021).

———. 1954. *The First and Last Freedom* (Foreword by Aldous Huxley). New York, Harper.

———. 1961. *Commentaries on Living*. Third Series. London, Victor Gollancz Ltd.

———. 1967. *J. Krishnamurti Talks in Europe 1967*. 1st Public Talk Paris April 16, 1967. http://legacy.jkrishnamurti.org/krishnamurti-teachings/viewtext.php?tid=18&chid=591&w=+dehumanization+of+society (accessed on 4 June, 2021).

———. 1972. A Discussion Meeting with the Teachers at Rishi Valley, February 9, 1967, *Krishnamurti Foundation India Bulletin*, Volume 1: Pp. 2–8.

———. 1973a. To the Schools. *Krishnamurti Foundation India Bulletin*, Volume 3: Pp. 12–14.

———. 1973b. Freedom and Discipline. Chennai, *Krishnamurti Foundation India Bulletin*, Volume 4: Pp. 15–16.

———. 1978. Letters to the Schools. https://jkrishnamurti.org/content/chapter-6-human-being-whole-mankind/a%20human%20being%20psychologically%20is%20the%20whole%20of%20mankind (accessed on 9 June, 2021).

———. 1982. Krishnaji Answers Questions. Madras, December 31, 1981. Chennai, *Krishnamurti Foundation India Bulletin*: Pp. 14–23.

———. 1985a. Talk to Invited Audience on the 40th Anniversary of the United Nations, New York April 1985. http://legacy.jkrishnamurti.org/krishnamurti-teachings/view-text.php?tid=1644&chid=1339&w=United+Nations+Talk (accessed on 9 September, 2021).

———. 1985b. *1st Public Talk*. Washington, DC. http://legacy.jkrishnamurti.org/krishnamurti-teachings/view-text.php?tid=34&chid=358&w=1st+public+talk+20th+April+1985%2C+Washington+DC (accessed on 9 September, 2021).

———. 1987a. *Krishnamurti's Journal*. London, Victor Gollancz Paperbacks.

———. 1987b. *Life Ahead*. Ojai, Krishnamurti Foundation of America.

———. 1993. *A Timeless Spring. Krishnamurti at Rajghat*. Chennai, Krishnamurti Foundation India.

———. 1995. 'If I were Head of Rishi Valley School'. International Trustees Meeting, Brockwood, September 11, 1984. Chennai, *Krishnamurti Foundation India Bulletin*, Volume 3: Pp. 20–21.

REFERENCES

———. 2000a. *All the Marvellous Earth* (co-editors Evelyne Blau and Mark Edwards). Ojai, Krishnamurti Foundation of America and Krishnamurti Foundation Trust (UK).

———. 2000b. Krishnamurti in Dialogue with Students at Rishi Valley, Change Yourself. 22 January, 1971. *Krishnamurti Foundation India Bulletin*, Volume 1: Pp. 14–15.

———. 2004. *On Freedom*. Chennai, Krishnamurti Foundation India.

———. 2011. Discussion on Education is the Responsibility of the Educator and the Parents. Rishi Valley, December 4, 1979. *Krishnamurti Foundation India Bulletin*, Volume 9, Issue 1, November 2011–February 2012: Pp. 3–27.

———. 2016. *Insights into Education. Bringing about a Totally New Mind*. Ojai, CA, Krishnamurti Foundation of America.

———. 2017a (1973). *The Awakening of Intelligence*. Chennai, Krishnamurti Foundation India.

———. 2017b (2007). A Nucleus of People Committed to the Teachings. In *Don't Make a Problem of Anything. Discussions with J Krishnamurti*. Chennai, Krishnamurti Foundation India. Pp. 3–23.

———. 2018a (1974). *On Education*. Chennai, Krishnamurti Foundation India.

———. 2018b. The Beauty of Silence. Chennai, *Krishnamurti Foundation India Bulletin*, Volume 15, Issue 2, July–December 2018: P. 2.

———. 2019a (1953). *Education and the Significance of Life*. Chennai, Krishnamurti Foundation India.

———. 2019b (1982). *Questions and Answers*. Chennai, Krishnamurti Foundation India.

———. 2019c. *Identity, Violence and Transformation*. Rishi Valley, Rishi Valley and Krishnamurti Foundation India Gathering. Pp. 1–59.

———. 2020. Nationalism, War and Peace. Chennai, *Krishnamurti Foundation India Bulletin*, Volume 17, Issue 2, July–December 2020: Pp. 4–15.

———. 2021. Why Are You Being Educated? Talk to the Students of Rishi Valley School, November 9, 1973. *Krishnamurti Foundation India Bulletin*, Volume 18, Issue 1, January to June 2021: Pp. 3–26.

Krishnamurti, J., and David Bohm. 1985. *The Ending of Time*. New York, Harper.

Krishnan, B.J., and Chaitanya Krishnan (compiled and edited) 2017. *F.G. Pearce. The Educationist*. Ooty, The Blue Mountains Publishers.

Kumar, Krishna. 1991. *Political Agenda of Education. A Study of Colonialist and Nationalist Ideas*. New Delhi, Newbury Park and London, Sage.

REFERENCES

———. 1997. Mohandas Karamchand Gandhi (1869–1948). In Zaghloul Morsy (ed.) *Thinkers on Education*, Volume 2. Delhi, UNESCO Publishing and Oxford and IBH Publishing. Pp. 507–515.

———. 2001. *Prejudice and Pride: School Histories of the Freedom Struggle in India and Pakistan.* New Delhi, Penguin.

———. 2015. Texts and Values. In Meenakshi Thapan (ed.) *Education and Society. Themes, Perspectives, Practices.* Oxford in India Readings in Sociology and Social Anthropology. New Delhi, Oxford University Press. Pp. 345–357.

———. 2016. *Education, Conflict and Peace.* Hyderabad, Orient Blackswan Ltd.

Kuyper, Marina. 2014. We Have a Good Philosophy, But Often it Gets Lost in a Lot of Words, Interview with Radhika Herzberger, 2008. In *Inspired by Krishnamurti. 10 Frank Interviews.* Netherlands, Milinda Publishers and Synthese. Pp. 39–51.

Lee, Mark R.E. 2015. *Knocking at the Open Door. My Years with J. Krishnamurti.* New Delhi, Hayhouse Publishers.

———. 2019. *World Teacher. The Life and Teachings of J. Krishnamurti.* New Delhi, Hayhouse Publishers.

———. 2020. *J. Krishnamurti's Process: Probing the Mystery.* Ojai, Edwin House Publishing.

Levinson, Bradley A., and Dorothy C. Holland. 1996. The Cultural Production of an Educated Person: An Introduction. In Bradley A. Levinson, Douglas E. Foley, and Dorothy C. Holland (eds.) *The Cultural Production of the Educated Person. Critical Ethnographies of Schooling and Local Practice.* Albany, State University of New York Press. Pp. 1–55.

Locke, John. 1692. *Modern History Sourcebook John Locke (1632–1704). Some Thoughts Concerning Education, 1692* https://sourcebooks.fordham.edu/mod/1692locke-education.asp (accessed on 20 August, 2010).

Lutyens, Mary. 1975. *The Years of Awakening.* New York, Avon Books.

———. 1983. *The Years of Fulfilment.* New York, Farrar, Strauss and Giroux.

———. 1988. *The Open Door.* London, Murray.

Mahmoudi, Sirous et al. 2012. Holistic Education: An Approach for 21 Century. *International Education Studies*, Volume 5, Issue 2, April 2012: Pp. 178–186. https://files.eric.ed.gov/fulltext/EJ1066819.pdf (accessed on 24 April, 2021).

Moody, David Edmund. 2017. *An Uncommon Collaboration. David Bohm and J. Krishnamurti.* Ojai, Alpha Centauri Press.

REFERENCES

Myrdal, Gunnar. 1968. *Asian Drama. An Inquiry into the Poverty of Nations*. London, Allen Lane The Penguin Press.

Neruda, Pablo. n.d. The Wide Ocean. www.pablonerudapoems.com/the-wide-ocean/ (accessed on 10 November, 2019).

Nussbaum, Martha. 2015. Tagore, Dewey and the Imminent Demise of Liberal Education. In Meenakshi Thapan (ed.) *Education and Society. Themes, Perspectives, Practices*. Oxford in India Readings in Sociology and Social Anthropology. New Delhi, Oxford University Press. Pp. 65–80.

O'Connell, K.M. 2003. Rabindranath Tagore on Education. In *The Encyclopedia of Pedagogy and Informal Education*. https://infed.org/mobi/rabindranath-tagore-on-education/ (accessed on 8 July, 2021).

Partho. 2007. *Integral Education. A Foundation for the Future*. Pondicherry, Sri Aurobindo Society.

Peat, David F. 1996. *Infinite Potential. The Life and Times of David Bohm*. New York, Perseus Publishing and Helix Books.

Reardon, Betty A. 1988. *Comprehensive Peace Education. Educating for Global Responsibility*. New York, Teachers College Press and ERIC.

———. 2000. Peace Education: A Review and Projection. In R. Moon, M. Ben-Peretz, and S. Brown (eds.) *Routledge International Companion to Education*. London, Routledge.

———. 2001. *Education for a Culture of Peace in a Gender Perspective*. Paris, UNESCO.

Rinpoche, Samdhong. 2019. Keynote Address at the Annual Krishnamurti Gathering on 'Identity, Violence, Transformation' organized by the Rishi Valley Education Centre, November 2019, Rishi Valley, Andhra Pradesh.

Romano, Arthur, and Laura Simms. 2012. *Education for Peace. A Resource Guide for Educators and the Community*. Rutgers Newark Center for the Study of Genocide, Conflict Resolution and Human Rights. https://peacelearner.files.wordpress.com/2012/01/peacesummit3.pdf (accessed on 14 May, 2021).

Rousseau, Jean-Jacques. 1974. *Emile*. Translated by Barbara Foxley. Everyman's Library. London, J.M. Dent and Sons.

Scott, James C. 1985. *Weapons of the Weak. Everyday Forms of Peasant Resistance*. New Haven and London, Yale University Press.

Sen, Amartya. 1999. *Development as Freedom*. Oxford, Oxford University Press.

———. 2021. *Home in the World. A Memoir*. Milton Keynes, Allen Lane and Penguin Random House.

REFERENCES

Sibia, Anjum. 2006. *Life at Mirambika. A Free Progress School.* New Delhi, NCERT.

Snauwaert, Dale T. 2014. Preface. In Betty A. Reardon and Dale T. Snauwaert (eds.) *Betty A. Reardon. A Pioneer in Education for Peace and Human Rights.* Cham, Heidelberg, New York, Dordrecht, London, Springer. Pp. vii–xvii.

———. (ed.) 2019. *Exploring Betty A. Reardon's Perspective on Peace Education Looking Back, Looking Forward.* Switzerland, Springer Nature.

Sonkar, Madhulika. 2018. 'Right Relationship' between Teachers and Students. Ethnographic Unravelling of Krishnamurti's Ideas in Educational Practice. In Meenakshi Thapan (ed.) *J. Krishnamurti and Educational Practice. Social and Moral Vision for Inclusive Education.* New Delhi, Oxford University Press. Pp. 147–182.

Sundaram, Anjan. 2014. Documenting Proximity. In *Conversation with Aditi Sriram.* www.guernicamag.com/documenting-proximity/ (accessed on 25 October, 2021).

Tagore, Rabindranath. 1917. *Personality.* London, Macmillan & Co.

———. 1929. Ideals of Education. *The Visva-Bharati Quarterly*, April–July: Pp. 73–74.

Thapan, Meenakshi. 2006 (1991). *Life at School. An Ethnographic Study* (2nd edition). New Delhi, Oxford and New York, Oxford University Press.

———. 2018. Krishnamurti, Values and Education. In Meenakshi Thapan (ed.) *J. Krishnamurti and Educational Practice. Social and Moral Vision for Inclusive Education.* New Delhi, Oxford University Press. Pp. 3–41.

———. 2021. Understanding Krishnamurti's 'Silences'. *The India Forum*, May 19, 2021. www.theindiaforum.in/letters/debating-j-krishnamurti.

Williams, C.V. 2004. *Jiddu Krishnamurti. World Philosopher.* New Delhi, Motilal Banarasidass Publishers Private Limited.

Zwart, Willem. 2012. An Experiment in Self Observation. *Journal of the Krishnamurti Schools*, Issue 16. www.journal.kfionline.org/issue-16/an-experiment-in-self-observation (accessed on 3 January, 2021).

INDEX

action(s) 5, 10, 42, 45, 47, 61, 79; basis of our 92; and behaviour 62; certain pattern of 65; examine our 39; inspires our 91; on an ideological revolution 15; immediate 45, 55; instant 55; mass- 48; pattern of 65; that are divisive 35; that must not be fragmentary 42; total human 42
agency 49, 71; faith in the 6; of the human agent 16; of an individual 73; in the public domain 19; voice and 78
'agency' and 'moral' value 14
approach 9, 40, 41, 54, 68, 77; education 87; to education 56; fragmentary 42; holistic 5, 56, 67n10, 90; insightful 6; instrumental 1, 56; integrated 5, 43, 56; to learning 81; narrow and sectarian 39; towards others 84; pedagogic 62; reflective 5
Arendt, Hannah 36
astachal 80, 82; experience at 86n10
astral: plane 7, 8; travel 8
attention 18, 35, 45, 46, 51, 57, 58, 81, 86n9, 90, 91; care and 87; to emotions 59, 92; focused 56; to the pedagogic processes 19; quality of 87; of students 54; to the work of the rural education centre 84
At the Feet of the Master (J. Krishnamurti) 8
Aurobindo 22, 23, 26n5
authoritarian: assertions 63; and assertive 87; culture 73
authority 39, 53, 61, 63, 64, 73; to exercise 61; and power 63
awakening: of the *kundalini* 12n11; of the senses 52; of the 'true centre' 22
awareness 91; to bring about an 15, 84; bring an 3; and commitment 6; a sense of conscious 75; and sensitivity 84
Ayur Gyan Nyas 92

Balasundaram, S. 68, 69
'banality of evil' 36; *see also* Arendt, Hannah
Besant, Annie 7, 8, 10, 12n4, 16, 18, 69, 85n3
Besant Theosophical College 7, 12n4
Blavatsky, Helena 7, 12n6
Bohm, David 10

INDEX

Bourdieu, Pierre 31; *see also* 'habitus'
Bourdieu and Passeron 14; *see also* education
Brockwood Park School 90
Buddha 11
Buddhism 7

caste 15, 29, 32, 35, 44, 46, 82, 83; lower 39, 44; marks on their foreheads 46; status 63
Centre for Learning (CFL) 90, 91
challenge(s) 27, 33, 37, 40, 44, 87, 93; continue to 88; devoid of 79; environmental 44; facing the 92; greater 31, 67n2; of life 91; meet the 41; new 40, 41; respond to the 91; social 27, 83
change(s) 11, 37, 45, 46, 49, 52, 73; administrative shifts and 74; in attitudes 43; bringing about a 43; bringing about this 14; capabilities for 6; the capacity for 24; centre of the 52; the educational landscape 92; essential for 1; at a global level 19; inner renewal or 23; leading to 52; *miraculous* 66n1; mitigate and impede 47; necessity of 54; our relationship 39, 43; possible to 31; possibilities for 6, 16, 48; radically and permanently 7; and renewal 24; responsibility for 46; social 36, 50, 64; through engagement with others 14; transformative way to 15; and uncertainties 89; work for 39
child('s) 14, 21, 22, 24, 30, 32, 56, 62; abilities 56; consciousness 50; cultivates self-images 32; development 5; is embedded 32; to be engaged in living 57; existence 29; 'good' 14; 'goodness' 20; influence the 32; integrated development of the 29; looks out at the social world 32; marriages 89; potential 56; understanding of the world 32
childhood 21, 32
children('s) 5, 15, 16, 21, 23, 32, 43, 44, 46, 47, 48, 51, 53, 54, 55, 59, 60, 61, 63, 64, 66, 66–67n2, 71, 72, 73, 78, 79, 80, 81, 82, 83, 84, 85n5, 87, 90, 92; access to schools by all 29; all-round development 56; education 79; are encouraged to 45, 84, 90; are not only enclosed 32; belonging to 29; cultivated in 23; development of 56; drop-out figures for 71; emotional development of 58; engaging with the 54, 68; experience with 60; fate of 89; a global outlook among 22; hearts and minds of 50; in their pastoral care 78; lives of 62; mobile 89; of migrants 89; out-of-school girl 89; questioned the 47; related to 49; at Rishi Valley 43; in schools 51; takes a toll on 88; understand their emotions 91; working with 19, 56, 65; young 6, 20, 43, 51, 92
citizenship 50; good 23
climate change: activism 43
classroom(s) 18; active in 72; are dominated 71; elementary school 71, 73; encounter 79 cognitive 56; development 58; and technological aspects 29
collective: individual and the 19; entity 82; goals 59; movement 39; struggle 48; unconscious 51

103

INDEX

colonial: anti- 25; citizen 27; ideals 27; legacy 25; nightmare 17
colonialist: enterprise 25; interests 22
communication: between participants 76; 'compassionate' 78; interaction and 28; 'intimate' 49, 76, 78; weak 76
comparison 61, 64, 77
compassion 20, 56, 67n9, 81, 92; for the poor 45; pursuit of 23; which heals all sorrow 9
competition 44, 64, 77; or comparison 61; *see also* comparison
conditioning 53, 65, 66; aspects of 11; break out of this 11; familial 32; free of the 61, 73; freedom from 2; of knowledge 61; learning without 65; psychological 11
conflict 5, 30, 34, 38, 39, 47, 56, 77, 80; with another 4; armed 3; both within and without 42; contain 24; create 35; is inevitable 63; in ourselves 4; in relationship 48; psychological 38; resolution 3; and sorrow 57; systems that perpetuate 2; and violence 25
conformity 55; free from 65
consumption: excessive 38; mindless 49
consciousness 22, 91; act from a 24; about change 19; child's 50; content of 59; developing greater 19; educated 60; enrich the 83; nationalism in our 51; oppressor 37; part of our 32, 37; whole 23; wholeness to 92
critical discernment: quality of 50
cultural and historical: antecedents of identity 67n2; forces 31

cultural 'production' of the educated person 15
culture(s) 20, 25, 28, 36, 55, 79, 80, 81; authoritarian 73; and civilisation 28; classes 81, 83; of the colonised 27; creates the 79; different 32; to flourish 82; history and 22; indigenous 27; of informality and freedom 78; local 72; model 72; national 22; other 72; popular 38; and religion 25; school 20, 80; at school 61; of the school 62, 79; that is open to questioning 82; tolerance for other 72; traditional 72; various 15
curriculum 50, 71, 83, 92; community-based 71; content of the 28; design 73; development 88; enrich the 19; essential aspect of the 54; with local knowledge 19; reinforced through the 54; at Santiniketan 22

Dalai Lama 91, 92, 93n6
'dependent origination' 91
Dharampal 27, 28
dialogue 10, 63; conversations and 63; around education 51; educational methods such as 5; engaging in 74; and observation 91; quality of 34; space for 82; a spirit of 78; with students 45
digital divide 89
discipline 61, 64, 65
'disposition', intersectionality is a 83
diversity: ecological 85n4; open to 2, 65; into school life 83; in the student population 79

earth 14, 16, 19, 21, 22, 30, 32, 35, 41, 43, 52, 68, 92; attitudes towards the 43–44; care for the 48; caring for the

44, 45; and humanity 19; loved the 44; nurture the 44; planet 49; things of the 44; wasteful using up of the 43
"earth nationalism" 44; *see also* "green culture"
earth's resources: misusing the 44
education 17, 18, 21, 22, 24, 25, 28, 40, 41, 43, 49, 50, 51, 52, 55, 56, 57, 58, 64, 68, 70, 76, 79, 82, 85n5, 87; alternative form of 22; approach to 5, 6, 90; appropriate 8; based on humanistic values 20; basic 24; change and 23; civic 27; cognitive and technological aspects of 29; as colonialist enterprise 25; to the communities 29; community-based model of 72; conventional 8; crafts-based 24, 25; dedicated to 69; dialogue around 51; different 55; distinctive 90; ethical foundations of 24; field of 18; for a 'good' child 14; holism in 43; holistic 19, 23, 56, 57, 77, 80, 92; and human development 59; idea of 28; 'importance of girls' 69; inclusive 70; Indian 27, 66n1; 'integral' 22, 59, 82; kit 71; lopsided 92; Macaulay's policy for 25; meaning of 34; 'modern' 27, 92; moral 27; 'national' 22; not fragmented 19; online 88, 89; potential of 2; practitioners of 6; promise that 2; psychological dimensions of a student's 23; purpose of 55, 74; 'right' 11, 29, 62, 68, 78, 87; right kind of 2, 40, 48, 80; role of 34, 50; rural 69, 70, 84, 85n5; secular 93n6; social and cultural reproduction through 14; as socialisation 28; social relations in 14; task of 43; teacher 88; technological aspects of 29; a 'transformational' peace 3; transformative potential of 2; tryst with 18; ultimate purposes of 75; understanding 1; views on 2; and violence 50
educational 42; aspirations 89; certification 12n9; co- 16, 79; context 54; endeavour 53, 69, 93; establishments 66n1; excellence 64; exercise 55; experience 17, 71, 89, 93; ideal 27; institution 68; institutions 19; integrated 16; knowledge 76; landscape 27; legacy 28; methods 5; model 23; resources 89; scenario 87, 90; setting 64, 75, 76, 81, 82; settings 27, 56; thought 3, 20, 26n6, 75; tools and pedagogic practices 28; transformation 62; vision 73, 91; work 29
educational practice 6, 51, 54, 59; aspects of 14, 29; component of 50; de rigeur in 58; freedom in 21; processes in 28; reproductive aspects of 14; within 51
Education as Service (J. Krishnamurti) 18
elementary 71, 73; children from 71; level in RVS 84; schools in India 85n5; structure for 71; *see also* school
emotional 56; competencies 58; concepts 39; development of children 58; learning 59; literacy 12n2; scaffolding 32; well-being 90
emotions: and behaviour 92; brought forth 25; engage

INDEX

with their 19; and feelings 48; manage their 59; mind and 8; one's thoughts and 60; to pay attention to 92; paying attention to 59; regulate his/her 92; and senses 20; that constitute the daily life of the school 29; and thought processes 91; and thoughts 91; understand our 61; understand their 91

empathy 81, 84, 92; engenders 20; lacks 30; for others 59

equity 74, 83–84, 90; is essential 46; social 48; *see also* social justice

ethics 24, 51; character building and 24; embedded in 24; of a new way of life 51; personal 52; pursuit of 49; universal 93n6

ethos 81; create an 61; maintaining an 82; of peace 3; to provide an 20; that constitutes school culture 64

examination(s) 12n9; 'cheating' to pass 71; passing of 52, 85n8; reproduced in 71; single 18

experience(s) 17, 18, 20, 71, 74, 75, 82, 83, 90; of beauty 58; of being different 63; to build the 83; children to 83; with children 60; in childhood 32; 'difference' 84; during the pandemic 89; freedom to 33; of going beyond the self 83; of interconnectedness 20; intimate 83; and lived realities 83; it viscerally 42; life-changing 9; of pain 37; a pleasant 60; previous 41; range of 5; reflective essay on the 60; regurgitates 37; relive their 80; at the school 90; 'vicarious' 33; weight of 62; a whole range of 5

faith: in the agency of the human subject 6; in an alternative system 39; blind 24, 28; family shapes the 32; free from 39; in an ideology 38; implicit 66–67n2; is a 'weapon of the weak' 39; in the path of *ahimsa* 25; in a religion 39; special 76; unerring 23; in the vastness of human potential 6

family 32, 41, 66–67n2; conditioned by the 32; experience in the 73; in the lap of the 73

fear 62, 63, 73; any form of 65; bound by 76; free of 77; grounded in 61, 73; hatred and 35; make children 61; or prejudice 63; without 16, 64

First and Last Freedom, The (J. Krishnamurti) 11

freedom 20, 21, 22, 29, 33, 37, 45, 55, 64, 65, 66, 73; absolute 63; in approaching 'truth' 11; articulate 66; atmosphere of 64, 80; from conditioned thinking 2; from conditioning 2; and cooperation 91; core of this 66; dimensions of 63, 76; and discipline 64; diversity and 20; emphasis on 21; enable 70; exercise of 21; and a form of human intelligence 2; fostering of 73; of the human subject 29; in itself 21; in the spirit of 91; individual 70; informality and 78; is a quality of the mind 65; of moral communion 21; no absolute 63; and order 29; in a particular sense 12n1; political 2; to reason

21; significance of 21; spirit
of 91; sustaining 34; towards
10; understanding of 66;
unrestrained 21; very little 77
'freedom cannot exist without
order' 64
Freire, Paulo 37
Froerer, Peggy 67n8

Gandhi, M.K. 24, 25, 26n6
general dispositions 31; *see also*
'habitus'
global outlook 92; development
of a 49; nurturing a 22;
students develop a 19
goals 28, 31, 80; attitudes and
20; collective 59; commitment
to 6; fulfilling their 70;
movement for 35, 51; of the
school 76; steadfastness of 87
good society 23; to flourish 2;
peace as a consequence of the
22; pursuit of the 23
"green culture" 44; *see also*
"earth nationalism"
Guindy School 69
Gupta, Latika 66–67n2

'habitual patterns': free of the 66
'habitus' 31
Herzberger, Hans and Radhika
Herzberger 68, 69, 80
Herzberger, Radhika 6, 19, 25,
34, 35, 51, 52, 54, 70, 74, 75,
80, 81
Hind Swaraj 24
human being(s) 2, 5, 6, 15,
16, 38, 43, 48, 51, 56, 74; a
complete 56; different kind
of 48; essential goodness of
55; fragmented 40; fellow
11; integrated 11, 19, 38, 56;
natural goodness of all 35, 51;
mutually interdependent 82; a
new generation of 61, 68, 73; a

new kind of 76; responsibility
of 35, 41; responsible as a 43
humanity 7, 38, 43, 44;
commitment for 3; concern
for 90; earth and 19;
interconnectedness of 49;
larger 35; with nature and
the planet earth 49; opening
out of the self towards 20;
repository of all 23; rest of 5,
10; restoring humanism to 50;
shared 92; united in our 35;
web of 35; whole of 52
Huxley, Aldous 10, 11

ideal(s) 79; colonial 27; of the
colonial citizen 27; are a
hindrance 56; rooted in an 56;
state of such communication
78; such as tolerance 72; way
of life 44
idealistic: perspective 56;
presentation of education 14
identification(s) 31, 33–34, 51;
break our 37; challenging
identity and 37; deepest sense
of 30; enhances the sense of
51; give up our sense of 49;
with ideas 34; with something
or someone 33; with the self
30, 34, 37; with thought 61;
and violence 37, 51
'identification with' 30, 33
identity(ies) 30, 31, 32, 35,
50, 67n3; attachment to
35; cannot be encased 32;
challenging 37; clinging to
35; consuming 49; cultural
and historical antecedents of
66–67n2; do away with 33,
35; essence of 32; express our
32; fluidity to 32; forming our
37; group 35, 83; healthy 59;
is not a fixed idea 82; own
88; issues of 82; in movement

32; questioning their own 88; scatter it in our 33; of the 'self' 92; sense of 32, 34, 37; student explorations of their 88; well-established 54; whole 32

ideological 31, 46, 74; aims 4; or mechanical enterprise 83; moorings 10; resolution to the problem 45

ideology(ies) 4, 33, 39, 65; achieved through any 1; adherence to a particular 1; as a crutch 39; divisive 48; faith in an 39; of 'non-violence' 38

'If I were Head of Rishi Valley School' 53

'imaginative sympathy' 23

inequality(ies): brought about a form of 28; caste, gender or class 46; of different kinds 39; economic and social 23; gender 47; hierarchy and 14; and misery outside the school 83; pervasiveness of 45; and violence against women 47; *see also* injustice

injustice: deep 45; through education 5; in every form of human relationship 45; movement against 39; seek to end 45; social 83; social trauma and 83; victims of 45

intelligence 80, 81; great deal of 4; human 2; moral 74

interaction: classroom encounter and 79; in the house 79; human 89; modes of 28, 62; open quality of 63; relationship develops through 78; sustained 72

interconnectedness 92; experience of 20; forms of 35

'interdependence' 91, 92

'intimate communication' 49; a spirit of 78; process of 76

justice 45, 66, 90; against 45; global 3; as keepers of 37; to the poor 37; social 3, 74, 83, 84; *see also* injustice

Kakar, Sudhir 31
Kaplan, Robert 44
Kishbaugh, Alan 66
knowledge 50, 55; academic 40, 57, 58; accumulation of 57, 58, 81; *acquisition and application* of 59; acquisition of 52; armed with 71; base of all 24; conditioning of 61, 73; conventional 40; created by 54; education based on building 52; embodied in 81; excessive 43, 54; focus on 55; forms of 24, 27; modern truth and 22; indigenous 27; legitimate 81, local 19; 'modern' forms of 27; prior 43; regurgitated 2; reproduction of that 40; reproduction of 76; skills and 19; and skills 40; subject-based 21; a wider 72

Krishnamurti Foundation India (KFI) 16, 17, 68, 73, 85n5, 88, 91

Krishnamurti school(s) 29, 45, 53, 54, 64, 74; aims of the 19; challenge teachers in 88; do not merely 'teach' 62; essential to a 87; growing up at a 83; in India 87; practices in the 3; that hold out the promise 80; relationships in a 63; school culture in a 82

Krishnamurti's: approach 3, 4, 5, 6, 7, 14, 16, 17, 18, 44, 46, 49, 52, 56, 62, 63, 64, 65, 68, 70, 74, 78, 85n5; assertion 'you are the world' 75; biography 12n5; commitment to the ending of

global violence 34; concern with decay of values 6; death 12n11; early life 7; educational challenge 27; educational endeavour 93; educational perspective 14, 56, 76, 92; educational thought 20, 75; educational vision 14, 27, 78, 87, 88, 90, 91; effort was to bring about an awareness 15; emphasis on 'goodness' 23; the extreme violence 37; extraordinary life 12n5; father 12n7; first school 16; focus on inclusive education 70; greatest concerns 30; life 6, 7, 8, 9; lifetime 67n6; most impassioned pleas 43; oft-cited statement 52; oft-quoted statements 75; own educational experience 17; perspective 11, 51, 56; profound legacy in education 50; the 'religious' mind 54; rich legacy 74; talks were banned 11; teachings 6, 12n8, 74; thought 77, 87, 90; underlying concern 52; use of 'thought-feeling' 91; views on education 2; vision 25, 62, 64, 74, 93; visits to other educational institutions 19; voice for a distinctive education 90; world view 76
Krishnamurti Study centres 17
Kumar, Krishna 12n3, 26n6, 27, 67n7, 85n7
Kumaraswamy, A. 73

Leadbeater, C.W. 7, 8
'Learning Ladder' 72
Lee, Mark 12n11, 17, 18, 52, 53
'long vision' 62; ensures the teacher's 62
Lutyens, Mary 12n5, 12n8

Macaulay's Minute on Education in India (1835) 26n7
memory 11, 37, 40, 54; acquires a sacred dimension in their 80; of being hurt 54; burden of 2, 43, 81; cultivating and strengthening 41; cultivation of 55; is a significant process 37; layer of 41; role of 43; that regurgitates experience 37; of violence 37
mind(s) 4, 14, 22, 33, 37, 43, 51, 53, 55, 60, 62, 63, 65, 66, 74, 82, 88, 91; conditioned 41; created by knowledge alone 54; 'creative' 54; of educators 89; and emotions 8; a fixation for things of the 24; 'free' 63; is free from conformity and can 'learn' 65; free of any form of fear 65; is memory 40; is the product of the past 40; a non-fragmented 65; oneness of the human 49; in our social environment 21; scientific 55, 56; shackles of the 10; that has been well put together 57; that is not cluttered 54; transformation of the human 50; workings of your own 66; and the world 21
morality: development of a 20; as the foundation of 25; secular 20, 24
movements: change through mass 48; disavowed all 40; one's psychological 22; open to the changing 32
Multigrade-Multilevel (MGML) 71, 73, 84, 85n5
Myrdal, Gunnar 66n1

nation(s) 32, 39; constitutes a 50; context of a single 50;

different 4; establish the 51; heterogeneous 23; hypocrisy of 4; idea of a 50; -state 51
national 41; anthem 12n4; boundaries 20; cultures 22; identities 31; ideology 35; politics in India 85n3
National Curriculum Framework 2005 71
nationalism 20, 25, 35, 49, 50, 52, 55; did not pave the way for peace 25; "disease" of 25; entrenched in 4; as a narrow cause 23; and organised religion 34
National Sample Survey Report on Education (2017–2018) 88
Neruda, Pablo 33, 67n3
non-violence 3, 38
Nussbaum, Martha 23

Oak Grove School 52, 53, 60
Olcott, Henry Steel 7
order 27, 29, 33, 35, 45, 50, 64, 73, 76, 78; a different world 39; to 'find out' for oneself 66; freedom and 29, 34; social 3; virtue is 29; in yourself 29
Order of the Star 10; dissolved the 9

pandemic: aftermath of the 89; COVID-19 88, 93n1; educational aspirations post- 89; education in the 88; imposed by the 89–90; triggered by the 89; vagaries of the 89
pastoral care 78, 88; *see also* children
Pathashaala 17
peace 1, 3, 4, 5, 11, 22, 90, 93; aims to bring about 93; 'authentic' 3, 25; beginning of 4; components for 5; education 3, 5, 12n3; education for 3, 5, 12n2, 89; educator for 2, 3, 25; to establish 2; global 5; and harmony on the planet 19; justice and 66; lasting 39; to live with 38; love of 74; moment of 2; 'negative' 3; pave the way for 25; pedagogies for 12n3; personal education for 12n2; posibilities for 20; 'positive' 3; practitioners of 6; proponent of world 83; seek to bring about 5; understanding 3; and well-being 2; in the world 2
Pearce, F.G. 75, 80
pedagogic 17, 63; approach 62; consequences 89; device that students use 85n8; method 71, 84, 85n5; practices 28, 51; processes 19
pedagogy 88, 89; essential part of educational 3; important component of 59
potential 60; a child's 56; human 6; of human beings 2; and purpose of the human subject 23; transformative 2
power(s) 25, 33, 36, 48; of education 21; freedom of 20; non-reducible form of 36; pursuit of 48; a range of psychic 7; structures of 15
prejudice 41, 55; without fear or 63, 67n2
process(es) 6, 14, 22, 24, 28, 30, 31, 34, 49, 59, 76, 81, 85n6, 87, 93; of the agency of the human agent 16; of becoming 33; of change 35, 51; of constructing the self 28; of education 14; educational 5, 16, 24, 34, 55, 73, 74;

INDEX

education as the *sine qua non* for 16; that engender development 70; entire 8; essentially a thought 33; of exclusion 50; external 24; of the imagination 51; is important 62; inner 38, 51; learning 72; of learning 82; of the mind 37; partake of a 79; and practices 31; psychological 1, 8; a significant 37; a simple 49; of socialisation 28, 32; of synthesis 31; of transformation 50; of understanding themselves 15; understand the 51; unfolding of the 62; unitary 42; unravel the 50; unusual 8; of watching the self 49; of working with children 51

'process, the' 8, 12n11

psychological 1, 8, 22, 38, 62; conditioning 11; demands that condition thought 2; development 58, 64, 77; dimension of individual life 6; dimensions of a student's education 23; processes 22, 31, 55, 64

'psychological revolution' 48

quality 2, 41, 54, 55, 65, 88; of affection 54; appreciate this 80; of care and attention 87; of critical discernment 50; of exploration 54; of immediate action 55; justice or 45; of looking 41; of relationships 80; of silence 80; of stillness and silence 81; of stillness that quietens the mind 82; of teachers 29

Rajghat Besant School 16, 19
Reardon, Betty 3, 5, 12n3

relationship(s) 2, 4, 11, 15, 28, 39, 45, 49, 52, 54, 57, 59, 61, 62, 63, 66, 70–78, 90, 92; authoritarian 44; based on authoritarianism and privilege 63; are the basis of an ethos 64; between adults and children 63–64; between education and violence 50; between the individual and society 14; between texts and values 85n7; 'a complex interlinking of' 92; comprehend our 20; as critical to the process of education 14; and curriculum 54; developing 60; to each other 43; with the earth 44; to the earth 44; individual's 23; that inhere at school 62; inquiry in and through 29; intimate 38; to knowledge 28; lack of 44; with nature 44, 45; network of 19; nuances of 82; to one another and to the world 82; with other human beings 38; with others 30, 41; to our closest kin 44; to people 43, 57; 'right' 11; self-inquiry and 5; to society 15, 23; teacher-student 63; understanding oneself in 10; utilitarian 44; within school 81; workings of the external world in 39; with the world 39, 91

religion 1, 9, 12n6, 24, 25, 29, 30, 33, 35, 52, 53, 54, 66–67n2, 83, 92; children are cynical about 54; circumscribed by the 32; circus of 54; faith in a 39; family's 66–67n2; fundamental premise of 9; organised 34, 53; and religiosity 53; spirit of 54

religious 10, 31, 56; action 42; activity 42; affiliations 49; attitude 24; barriers 22; communities 29; creeds 21; diktats 20; divisions 15; education 57; identity 66–67n2; ideology or practice 55; lives 53; moorings 40; prejudices 41; qualities 54; spirit 54, 55, 57; teacher of the greatest distinction 11; way of life 53; *see also* mind
'religious education' 52
responsibility 5, 15, 23, 41, 42, 43, 46, 64, 73, 75; of acting individually 1; and an action 42; attention to one's 46; to care about the world 52; complete 52; for the earth 15, 30, 44, 48; to the earth 35; towards the earth 43; to first 'put one's house in order' 46; of individuals to society 14; lies at the core of this freedom 66; towards nature 43; personal 66; to the rest of humankind 16; sense of 15, 21, 62, 75; sense of oneness and 5; as social beings 3; for the world 2, 9
revolution 48; act of 66; in man's thinking 42; organising a 1; seek a social 47; violent 48
Right to Education (RTE) Act (2009) 72
Rinpoche, Samdhong 36, 49, 78, 85n2
Rishi Valley 16, 17, 19, 43, 68, 69, 70, 71, 74, 75, 78, 80, 84, 85–86
Rishi Valley Education Centre (RVEC) 3, 6, 68, 69, 70, 84
Rishi Valley Institute of Educational Resources (RIVER) 72–73; initiated its pedagogic method 71

Rishi Valley School (RVS) 34, 45, 51, 53, 54, 57, 63, 68, 69, 73–84
Rishi Valley Special Development Area (RVSDA) 85n4
rural education 70; centre 69, 84; work for 85n5
rural education programme: Rishi Valley's 70

sacred: dimension 80; 'place' 68
Sahyadri School 17
sameness: recognition of this 4; sense of 31
Santiniketan 12n4, 21, 22, 26n4
Satellite Schools 71
school 11, 15, 19, 26n5, 27, 53, 60, 61, 62, 64, 69, 70, 73, 74, 75, 76, 78, 80, 83, 85n5, 85n8, 86, 87, 88, 90, 91, 92, 93, 93n1; ability of 20; absent from 77; academic learning in 56; academic subjects at 15; access to 29; 'alternative' 79; bad time at 18; beyond the 15; children at 16; children in 51; co-educational 16, 79; culture at 61; cultural context of a 20; culture of the 79; curricula 50, 91; daily life of the 29; day 16, 77, 81, 82; a day-boarding 17; education 21, 29, 59, 91; an elite 63; establish a 52; ethos 81; extended to spaces outside 15; fee-paying 73, 85n5; foundations to run his 11; freedom in any 63; functioning of the 77; government and private 71; Handbook 77; across India 58; in India 25, 47, 50; just the 15; in Krishnamurti's direction 87; Krishnamurti's first 16; life 75, 77, 79, 81, 82, 83, 84, 86n9, 88; life at 34, 77, 79, 84, 86n9; like-minded 91; misadventures

112

INDEX

in 18; NDMC 67n2; oldest 16, 68; participants in 77; *Patha Bhavan* 26n4; personnel 29; practice(s) 87, 88; primary and secondary 23; private 71; processes 79; reproduces society 28; residential 17, 68, 78, 79; role of the 32; routine 77, 81, 82; senior 84; single teacher schools 71; small 17, 90, 91; space of the 28; spaces outside 15; success in 58; Tagore's 21; uniform 77; a unique feature of the 17; website 90, 91; work 84; around the world 2

school culture 20, 64, 74, 79, 80, 81, 83, 85n8, 87; at the heart of the 77; in a Krishnamurti school 82; nuanced 80

School in a Box 71

schooling 28, 82; competitive 63; education and 18; for Krishnamurti 17; memories of his 18; process 76; processes 76; *see also* curriculum; education

scientific: and religious spirits 56; mind 55, 56; spirit 55

Scott, James C. 39

secular: education 93n6; morality 20, 24

self 92; attachment to the 30; beyond the 30, 83; boundaries of the 82; constitution of the 28; constructing the 28; extension of the 31; focus on the 42; free of the 30; grows tougher and more capable 33; higher 30; individual 29; movement of the 30; objectively 'real' 33; opening out of the 20; perpetuation of the 34; 'real' 30, 33; supreme 30; robust sense of 33; understanding of the 41; watching the 49; within a group 31

self-abandonment: total 58

self-aggrandisement: goals devoid of 6

self-awareness 59

self-centred 30, 61; attitudes and goals 20; understanding 64

self-criticism: Socratic 23

self-destructive world 49

self-identification 30; doing away with 42; forms of 49, 50; a strong sense of 25

self-inquiry 5, 10, 14, 48, 49, 62, 90; into one's consciousness 59; process of 5, 30, 59

self-interest and self-perpetuation 35, 51; *see also* self

self-knowledge 22, 43, 57, 59; deep 60; process of 76

self-perpetuation 35, 51; *see also* self

self-understanding 11; by teachers and students 58

Sen, Amartya 21, 85n6

sensitivity 58, 84, 87

Shaw, George Bernard 11

Shibumi 91

Sholai school 90

Social, Emotional, and Ethical (SEE) Learning programme 92

social change 36, 50; individual and 64

Social Emotional Learning (SEL) 58, 59

social institutions 32, 36, 39

social justice: bringing about 84; equity and 74, 83, 84; positive implementation of 3; *see also* justice

social media: frequent use of 88

social world 32, 83; just 16, 82

society 24, 25, 35, 37, 39, 45, 46, 50, 51, 55, 66n1, 84;

capitalist 38; civil 49, 70; contemporary 51; cowed down by 14; creating a 24; de-humanisation of 38; democratic 23; disadvantaged and marginalised sections of 84; divisiveness in 20; of equals 48; foundation of a new 23; individual and 14, 22; inequities in 83; just equitable 20; massification of 38; more humane 20; order in 34; productive member of 35; renewal of 51–52; responsible member of 23; school curriculum emphasises a particular 50; transform 39; transformation in 52; transformation of 6, 14; transformative ways to change 15; values in 6; virtuous 14; well-being of 2, 28; without 'national economic divisions' 23
sorrow 16, 37, 39, 42, 57; ending of 18; heals all 9
'stream of consciousness' 60; as thought-feeling 59; *see also* thought-feeling
Subba, Rao G.V. (GVS) 69

Tagore, Rabindranath 12n4, 20, 21, 22, 26n4
'teachings, the' 73
textbooks 18, 71, 87; culture in India 85n7; dominated by teachers and 71; Indian and Pakistani 67n7; reliance on 71; is the ruler of consciousness 71; studies of history 50; with uniform content 72; teaching is through the 71
The School KFI 16
Theosophical Society 7, 9, 10, 12n7, 16, 26n2, 85n1

Theosophy 7–10, 12n6
'thought-feeling' 59–61, 91; *see also* 'stream of consciousness'
transcendental and local orders 76–77
transformation 6, 14, 16, 36, 41, 43, 47, 48, 49, 50, 51, 52, 60, 76; of consciousness and social change 50; of healing and 51; of the human mind and consciousness 50; political agenda for social 1; practitioners of peace and 6; radical 23; self-inquiry and social 14
'translocation': to emphasise the transcending of local or national boundaries 19–20
truth 9, 58; 'freedom' in approaching 11; is a pathless land 9; not ignore modern 22; representative of 81

'Universal Ethics' 91, 92
University of California, Berkeley 19

value(s) 21, 74, 76; are shared 74; bringing in 92; in the curriculum 74; decay of 6; for a democratic society 23; ethics and 24; of humanism 22; humanistic 20; intellectual 48; of life 6; 'moral' 14, 53; of peace and harmony 20; sensate 2; texts and 85n7; that Krishnamurti highlights 6
Valley School 17
Vasanta College 16
village communities 69; folk 70; youth 71
villagers 47, 69, 90
villages 48, 88, 89
violence 2, 3, 30, 37, 41, 43, 47, 49, 55, 67n4; acts of 50; against women 36, 47;

banality of 37, 49; bemoaning 1; caste-based 36; conflict as 38; directions of 36; a distinct phenomenon 36; domestic 36; education and 50; ending of 38, 39; everyday 51; excessive 6; extreme 37; fact of 36; field of 36; forms of 3, 36, 38; free from 16; free of 34; global 34; has become a market 36; hatred and 24; identification and 37, 51; inherent 43; justify 50; leads to 35; mob 36; opposition to 37; physical 41; perpetrators of 37; transaction of 51; unprecedented 36; visibility of 37; war and 35; within us 39

virtue 50, 65; is order 29; mediocrity as a 81; and personal ethics 52; petty 20

whole of life 35, 57
'wholeness of universal consciousness, the' 49
Woods National College 12n4; *see also* Besant Theosophical College
'World Teacher' 7, 8, 9, 10
'world university' 69

Zwart, Willem 60, 61

For Product Safety Concerns and Information please contact our EU
representative GPSR@taylorandfrancis.com
Taylor & Francis Verlag GmbH, Kaufingerstraße 24, 80331 München, Germany

www.ingramcontent.com/pod-product-compliance
Lightning Source LLC
Chambersburg PA
CBHW071822230426
43670CB00013B/2543